SIGN & THRIVE

HOW TO MAKE SIX FIGURES AS A
MOBILE NOTARY AND LOAN SIGNING AGENT

BY BILL SOROKA

ISBN: 978-1-7341833-0-6

DISCLAIMER

The results I have created in my mobile notary and loan signing business are not typical and should not be expected as "ordinary." In fact, the results I have obtained are extraordinary. Not because I am special. Not because I have some secret code or handshake that gets me all the business. I get extraordinary results from extraordinary effort. I do things differently from mainstream mobile notaries and loan signing agents and that's what I share in this book. In fact, if mainstream is what you are looking for, you've picked up the wrong book.

And, you might as well get used to this disclaimer too:

"I am not an attorney and may not give legal advice or accept fees for legal advice."

To get the best experience with this book, get access to the resource page. There is a ton of free resources provided for you! Get access at
www.notarycoach.com/freestuff

FREE RESOURCES INCLUDE:

- Training Links
- Product links
- Mortgage Document Downloads
- Replay Video Training
- Personal Development Links
- Accounting Software
- And more!

WHAT OTHER NOTARIES ARE SAYING ABOUT THIS BOOK

"Bill is on Fire! I am amazed at how he has taken the complex and made it simple. If you are looking for a book that will do more than teach you about the technical skills required to be a loan signing agent, then get ready. Bill will, step by step, show you how to implement critical strategies and skills in a way that will attract customers and turn them into *lifetime* clients. There are other notary books available, but none that focus on the mission of your business and relationship building. That is what will sustain and guide you for the long run! Whether you want to start a Notary Business, or you are already running one, but need momentum to grow it to its full potential, you have found the right tool to develop the business and lifestyle of your dreams. Bill's collaborative style and desire to be of service is demonstrated over and over as he shares everything you need to make your business successful…on your own terms."

—Laura J Biewer- CA Mobile Notary and Loan Signing Agent & Founder of CoachMeLaura.com

"Bill Soroka's Sign & Thrive book is a must read for anyone who is interested in notary work. It's your step by step guide, and easy reading. He's a champion of starting new businesses, and it's served him well. This book is an enjoyable read from start to finish, and full of all the information you need to start a new day, a new business, a new you."

—Bobbi Illing-AZ Mobile Notary and Loan Signing Agent, Real Estate Agent, and Writer

"Whether you are brand new to being a Notary Public or have been one for 30+ years, this book offers value to everyone. Bill Soroka is very relatable as he shares his journey in the industry. His book will draw you in and entertain, as well as educate you about the trials and tribulations as a Notary Public and Loan Signing Agent. You can make six figures in this industry, and Bill is just the guy to show you how. I have read and watched several training programs, but none have been as informative and influential as Sign and Thrive."

—Dorie McCleskey-CO Mobile Notary and Loan Signing Agent

"Who knew that someone holding the underestimated Office of a Notary Public could run a thriving business. Bill knew. He has taken the Office of the Notary Public and raised this public servant "job" to the level of the entrepreneur while still maintaining the integrity of the Office. He has provided a methodology that anyone can follow from obtaining the Notary Public Commission to a thriving self-supporting business. Along the road he weaves in many important concepts of running a business as well as reminding us of the vast importance of this office. Yet he does not forget the most important aspect of running a business, the self. Thus he reminds us of the importance of self-awareness and offers us a well-rounded list of options. He generously includes his success model, "The Daily Do's."

If you are thinking about becoming a Notary Public, newly commissioned, or seasoned with multiple commissions, Sign & Thrive is for you. Also, while Sign & Thrive is written for the Notary Public, many of the principles in this book apply to anyone just getting started in business. I highly recommend not just reading this book but taking to heart and action the principles and concepts presented."

—Valerie C. Dennis-TX Mobile Notary and Loan Signing Agent and Co-founder of Safe Haven for Notaries

"This book is absolutely a must-read if you want to be a well-informed Notary Signing Agent. Bill goes into depth about how to become a Notary Signing Agent, as well as to run a successful Mobile Notary and Notary Signing Agent business. This book is filled with many useful resources that will get you well on your way to start a successful entrepreneurial Notary and Notary Signing Agent business."

—Jason Braunstein-FL Mobile Notary and Loan Signing Agent and Co-founder of Safe Haven for Notaries

"Bill has an amazing way of writing informatively and concisely. He does not alienate the reader with too many industry terms. His writing comes from a place of compassion and a true calling to teach and mentor. He wants the reader to succeed and be the best version of themselves they are meant to be.

It's evident in the book's spirit. I highly recommend this to any persons looking to get into the mobile notary industry."

—Jennifer Denoia-Loan Signing Agent, Mortgage Underwriter, and Future Author

DEDICATION

Choosing who to dedicate this book to was one of the hardest decisions I've had to make in the whole process. I've been blessed with lots of love and support over the years, and that hasn't been easy for some. When you have as many failed businesses under your belt as I do, it can be exhausting as a friend, a lover, a parent, a sibling, or even as a business partner. Still, many stuck around, and for those who did (and even the ones who didn't), I am eternally grateful. But for this book, I decided to dedicate it to anyone who dares to hope that they can create a new life of possibilities for themselves. And since you're reading this, I'm dedicating this book to you. Being a mobile notary and loan signing agent has changed my life in ways I never even imagined. This work matters. And you can do it.

"Twenty years from now you will be more disappointed by the things you didn't do than by the ones you did do. So throw off the bowlines. Sail away from the safe harbor. Catch the trade winds in your sails. Explore. Dream. Discover."

—Sarah Frances Brown

"If we did all the things we are capable of doing, we would literally astound ourselves."

—Thomas Edison

ACKNOWLEDGMENTS

Well, we might as well start learning right away. As a Notary Public, "Acknowledgments" have a whole different meaning than normally intended at the Foreword of a book. In our notarial world, an acknowledgment is a formal decree from a signer that they are, or have, willingly signed a document. But you probably already know that, or you soon will.

However, there are still people I want to acknowledge in the traditional sense too. Acknowledgments are normally used to thank those who helped bring a book together.

Gratitude is the biggest attribute of success that there is. Whether you are feeling gratitude or expressing it to others, trust that this is the "magic" you are looking for. Your business, your life, begins to "pop" the minute you feel its heat. And if you find a way to express it, you'll be on the "express way" to success.

***

Mom, thank you for raising me with an open and creative mind that was encouraged to dream big and dream often. I have written and published this book because you told me I could do anything I wanted from a very young age.

Dad, I think you just kind of assumed I could do anything I put my mind to. Thank you for that.

Ali, your gentle push to complete this book has meant the world to me. Even when I resisted it, I have appreciated it. You've showed me what true love and caring is all about. Thank you.

Jeannie, it really all started with you telling me I should be a mobile notary. Thanks for hiring me first and triggering this whole adventure.

Chandler Bolt, you've built a business helping people like me release the story in their hearts. I hope you realize the power of your smile and your system. Thank you.

Hal Elrod, your book, The Miracle Morning, was life-changing for me, and I am so glad you found the courage to share your story. In fact, I measure my experience here on earth as life before The Miracle Morning, and life after The Miracle Morning.

Carol Ray & Laura Biewer, thank you for your open hearts and commitment to helping others achieve their greatness. I am grateful every day that our paths have crossed.

Jamie, thanks for the beer and the conversation that shifted my attention to this amazing business!

To the friends who stuck around, even when they didn't understand me- thank you for being there.

And, to both of my Grandmother's who didn't get to see this book published (on earth, anyway), thanks for putting up with my dreams and grandeur. I never did things the "old fashioned way." I had to do them my way. Even when you didn't understand or agree, you always loved and supported in your own way.

Thank you!

FOREWORD BY CAROL RAY, FOUNDER OF NOTARY2PRO

Bill asked me if I would be willing to write the Foreword for his new book, "Sign & Thrive: How to Make Six Figures as a Mobile Notary and Loan Signing Agent." I did not hesitate for one minute. I was very surprised that he asked me and told him I would be so honored to do this for him. Part of the reason is the story that brought us together.

My company "Notary2Pro" has been in business for ten (10) years this 2019. My goal was to train Notaries Public to become Professional Certified Notary Signing Agents. There was no comprehensive detailed training for this in this country and I wanted to "raise the bar" in this industry. The thousands of our graduates working today are proof that we have exceeded our expectations.

By the beginning of 2018 I began seeing a lot of people offer training to notaries to teach them how to become Notary Signing Agents. Each new teacher claimed to have the number ONE training course and claimed to provide students with the secret to making BIG money in this industry. I found out through the experiences of others that most of these people were not fulfilling the promises they advertised.

Here was another new trainer who called himself the "Notary Coach", always in his car, camera rolling, and he is sharing his ideas about how to be successful in this industry. There was something about Bill that drew my attention in a more positive way than with the others I had watched. So, after watching him for a while I called him on the phone. In my mind it was the question "Is he a good guy or is he out to take advantage of notaries who want to do this job and is only in it for the money?" Frankly, I did not get my answer the first time, nor even the second phone call but by the third call I felt a kindred spirit with this young man (about ½ my age). I could feel his passion for this industry, and he painted a very clear picture of how much he wanted to do to "raise the bar" just as I had 10 years earlier.

Bill and I got to know each other and found that we are very similar in our dedication to this business and to the notaries trying to learn to be the best they can be.

Bill and I created a project which began as the "Breakfast Club". We appeared via Zoom on computer screens all over the country. With a small following Bill and I would talk, answer questions and developed a relationship with our audience. Since then we invited a dear friend of mine, Laura Biewer to join us and renamed our little group "Tuesday Notary Titans" (TNT). We try hard to provide our growing audience with inspirational stories, information that will take our audience's businesses to another level and answer an unending amount of interesting questions. We three are teachers to our core and we three all care so much about the people in our industry.

Bill's book is filled with so much helpful information that, when used, will absolutely propel your business into a level of professionalism and success that you may have dreamed of but never thought possible. It is beautifully written and organized as well as any reference guide I have ever seen. He shares a lot about himself personally which automatically draws you to him as a person.

If you are reading this Foreword , you have this book and I want you to know that you will be wearing down each page because *every page* has a ton of information and is very valuable.

—Carol Ray

TABLE OF CONTENTS

INTRODUCTION

"There is nothing more powerful than an idea whose time has come."

—Victor Hugo

You probably picked up this book for one of two reasons: One, you're already a mobile notary (maybe even a current loan signing agent) and you want to continue learning, enhancing, and growing yourself and your business (which I love, by the way). Or, if that doesn't describe you, then you likely fall into reason number two; You have a longing inside for something different-something better or greater than your current circumstances. You're looking for a way to "reclaim your agenda" as my mentor, Brendan Burchard, says.

If you're like I was not too long ago, you probably have a feeling deep inside that you are destined for something better. Maybe you have a business you've always wanted to start, an invention you've always tinkered with, or a book you've always wanted to write. But then, life happened. Not necessarily a bad life, but circumstances that distracted you from your dream- marriage, kids, school, work.

But I don't think dreams ever really die. So even though we've been distracted, the call from destiny is still inside, no matter how muffled its sound. Eventually, the call gets louder, and louder. A slow rumble that eventually shakes you out of distraction. The idea of approaching the end of your life, or even the middle of it, without letting your idea, message, business, book (or whatever your masterpiece may be) manifest, is terrifying.

Why do I think that? I was there, too. I'll share more of that story in a minute. For now, know you are in the right place at the right time. Becoming a successful, thriving mobile notary and loan signing agent may very well be the vehicle you're looking for to make all your "big" dreams come true.

You see, this business isn't just about how to sign, date, and stamp a piece of paper. This business gives you liberty.

How does that happen?

This business stands on three main tenants that I've come to love and appreciate:

Flexible Schedule- Get your time back. Most people are so exhausted after working 9-5 for someone else that they cannot even imagine growing a business or pursuing a dream after hours.

Unlimited Income- You work. You get paid. Grow it. Expand it. Shrink it. Scale it. The choice is yours.

Legitimate Business- You're the last line of defense in identity and mortgage fraud. Own that. Be proud of that.

This isn't what I would call "easy" work. Simple, maybe, but not easy. Still, for the above-mentioned reasons, and so much more, this is a business you can work honorably, and still make time for your big dreams.

If I've done my job correctly, you'll be inspired to take this on and create the business and mindset that will carry you through to joy and success, however you decide to define it.

MY STORY

"If there is no struggle, there is no progress."

—Frederick Douglass

I've been an entrepreneur, at least in spirit, since the very beginning. As a kid, I wore fake glasses and carried around a giant, nerdy 1970's insurance-salesman-type briefcase, filled with "important papers." Forget the toy stores, take me to an office supply store! I could never have too many staplers, file folders, and…pens. This didn't do much for my social life as a child, but I just knew I wanted to be a business man when I grew up. That and a bus driver. And a psychologist. And an Indiana-Jones-level archeologist. And, the list goes on. I saw the potential in many things, just like I still do today.

I am a multi-potentialite serial entrepreneur. I know, it's a mouthful. Try fitting that on a business card. A multi-potentialite is someone with many interests, hobbies, and creative pursuits. My creative pursuits just happen to be, or turn into, businesses; hence, the "serial entrepreneur."

MISCONCEPTIONS

In total, I have about 26 or 27 businesses, ventures, or brands under my belt. The most successful of which, is the topic of this book. Interestingly enough, it's the one I had least hopes or expectations for. The idea that a Notary Public could make this much money had *never* occurred to me.

Who knew that notaries actually made money? Much less, earn multiple six-figure income?

Plus, even being a nerd, what I pictured notary life to be seemed pretty…boring. I mean, who would want to shuffle paper, the *same* paper, all day, every day. Not me! Sure, maybe I did want to be a business man, but I certainly didn't want to sit in an office or a cubicle all day. The road was calling me; it always has. I am a free spirit with big dreams and the personality to match. No way was I going to be a paper pusher. Plus, I had never been one for detail. I am a big picture guy. In my head, a Notary Public *must have to* be an even bigger nerd than me with an attention to detail that is too rare.

Nope, not for me.

I was *very* wrong about this. As a mobile notary and loan signing agent, I make considerable income. In fact, it's literally unlimited, like many other businesses. Plus, it's flexible, and I don't have to be confined to an office.

I get to be out on the open road, pretty much as long as I'd like to be. I get to go as far as I want. And yes, there is some attention to detail required, of course, but it's not to the level I had imagined. While there is definitely some minutia involved, every signing is different, because every person is different. And I think that's what gives me energy. I love the people I get to meet in this business. And, as an introvert, that's refreshing. As my friend Bobbi says, "we can like anyone…for an hour."-I really enjoy people and being of service, but I derive energy from being alone. This is the perfect balance for me- an hour or so with a client closely followed by an hour (or less) of private drive time.

HOW I GOT STARTED

I'll tell you all about how, and why, I got started. But first, let me give you some context, and part of the downside to being an undisciplined multi-potentialite. It all started when I was attempting to launch and manage 5 or 6 of the above-mentioned businesses *all at once*. One of the challenges a multi-potentialite serial entrepreneur must face, is this problem of too much opportunity and distraction. I learned that the hard way.

For the record, launching five companies on a shoe-string budget is not advisable. Even with a little traction in each, there just aren't enough resources. That's a book in and of itself though. The fact is, even with a little momentum, I wasn't able to survive. Every one of those business was an extra "mouth to feed." That left very little for me, so I couldn't pay myself. So, I *had* to create income to pay the bills.

In an effort to help me out, a family friend mentioned I should be a loan signing agent. She was an escrow officer and saw what a loan signing agent got paid, so it could be exactly what I needed. Looking for *any* way to avoid another call-center job or corporate nightmare, I jumped on it.

I had no idea what I was doing, but I dove in. I had no formal training at all. In fact, I knew of no training programs at all. I had to learn by experience alone. I thought I had discovered this all new career!

My escrow officer friend agreed to run through a few signings with me and throw me some business. Talk about stressful! 150-200 pages of loan documents, and I was supposed to know what each of them were *and* make sure the signer correctly signed, dated, and initialed, each one. The first few months were rocky, to say the least. Every signing pretty much gave me an ulcer:

- I was terrified someone was going to ask a question I couldn't answer.
- I was afraid I would see a document I didn't recognize and look like a fool.
- I knew I was in "fake it til you make it" mode and I was sure people could see right through me.

In order to make this business work, I needed a system and a script. I needed each signing to run just about the same, every time. At least for the part I could control. I created that system, and that is how the Sign & Thrive Notary Course and Community system came to be.

Here's the thing…every signing is different. You might memorize a script, have a system in place for everything you touch, but there is a factor that can't always be accounted for-people. There are people involved in every aspect of a real estate or mortgage transaction: borrowers, sellers, real estate agents, loan officers, closing agents, appraisers, inspectors, brokers, managers, and more. And since there are so many people involved, this leaves ample opportunity for human errors, personality conflicts, laziness, awesomeness, great conversation, sad circumstances, laughter, tears, anger, joy, and every other possible human emotion.

That's what makes this business interesting. There's an adventure around every signing. Some are smooth, efficient, and plain. Some are fun. Some are stressful. Some are intense. Most, are smooth and efficient when you apply the techniques in this book. Most of what I teach here are from hard lessons I had to learn. Remember, I didn't have a course or a mentor to show me what to do and what to avoid. I made lots of mistakes. They were expensive ones. Mistakes I hope to help you avoid when you read this book.

The ultimate message I can send to you is to treat your mobile notary and signing agent venture like the business that it is. There is tremendous opportunity here. And, if you respect it, appreciate it, and give it the attention it deserves, you'll thrive with it. My notary business has always been there when I needed it. If I needed to make $3,500, which I needed that first month as a notary, my business provided. If I needed to focus on all those other ventures, and only needed $1,000 that month, that's what I worked. The only reason this business ever got inconsistent results is when I put in inconsistent effort.

I treated my notary business like an ATM machine. I only worked it when I needed it to make money for my other ventures. One conversation changed all that.

Over a pitcher of beer with my friend, Jamie, she asked me a question that catapulted my life and business forward . I was down in the dumps because every business I had at the time, all five or six of them, were flopping. Jamie said, "What about the notary gig, Bill? It's the one business that seems to have always been there when you needed it. Why not apply everything you've learned to that business?"

She was right. I managed to have one or two clients that stuck with me, and I was able to earn about $1,000 a month consistently. Looking back, this seems like it should have been pretty obvious, but at the time it was ground-breaking, and I felt the lightbulb go on. I started focusing on the mobile notary and signing agent business. I started applying all the knowledge and lessons from a lifetime of entrepreneurship and commitment to personal growth.

I went from making $1,000 a month as a signing agent, to making over $20,000 a month within about 90 days. I wish I could say this was some difficult, highly involved system, but it really wasn't. All I did was implement standard marketing and relationship-building practices *consistently*.

This opportunity, as a mobile notary and loan signing agent flies under the radar in many ways. I think many, even seasoned notaries, take it for granted at times.

Many signing agents have not taken full advantage of the opportunity they have. They've adopted a "set it and forget it" business model. They'll get started, set up a few profiles, maybe a website, register for a few signing companies, and then sit back and wait for the phone to ring. Believe it or not, this actually works in some markets.

But, for real, extraordinary results, we require extraordinary effort.

WHY I WROTE THIS BOOK

I am not perfect. Far, far, far, from it. Every possible mistake a Notary Public, or small business owner could make, I made and often repeated.

Early in my mobile notary and loan signing business, I made some poor choices:

- I chose short-term gains over long term relationships.
- I marketed my services intermittently, only when I felt "inspired" to do so.
- I thought there was no way a client would ever fire me (holy ego, Batman!).
- I've spilled coffee on an entire set of *signed* documents.
- I've carelessly allowed a borrower to "under-sign" his signature on every single page.
- I've missed one signature on the single most critical document in a loan signing and had to drive back…four hours away.
- I've "quit" this business so many times that many of my friends didn't even know I was still a notary .
- I've disrespected this business, and some of the people in it, along the way.

Bridges were burned. Epic mistakes were made. Tens of thousands, and likely hundreds of thousands, of dollars have been lost. Even through all this, I not only survived, I thrived in this business as a mobile notary and loan signing agent.

With this book, you'll have a leg up- way more than I ever had. Maybe you can avoid some of the same pitfalls and mistakes I made and create your dream lifestyle faster than I did.

That's my hope for you.

THE COMPANION COURSE

I have created this book as a companion to the online course I have by the same name- The Sign & Thrive Notary Training Course and Community. There is no obligation to join the course, but within it, you will see a demonstration of my commitment to this idea of "kaizen," the Japanese philosophy of constant, continuous improvement.

There are hundreds of video modules that dive into the specifics of how to sign, date, stamp, and print documents, of course. But, there is also substantial material about how to grow yourself and build authentic relationships. It is a course designed to be everything you need to succeed in this business.

You can start a free trial to poke around at:

www.notarycoach.com/freestuff

HOW TO USE THIS BOOK

We all learn in our own ways. Do what's best for you. However, I want you to stay on track. To help with your learning, I have broken down the book into sections that mirror my Sign & Thrive Notary Training Course. Like the course, this book is totally flexible, too.

There is a lot of detail provided. I recommend you read the book from cover to cover and focus on the parts that need your immediate focus. If you have the print version, please write in the margins, underline what speaks to you, and fold page corners.

If you only have the digital version, grab a journal or a notebook that is reserved just for this book. As your own ideas come, write them down.

There are many paths to success in this business. I just happened to find a system that has earned me hundreds of thousands of dollars per year, and I enjoy sharing it with you. The results can be, and have been, replicated over the years, so I am not some anomaly in the industry.

That said, my results are not typical. There are too many variations that can affect outcomes. The most powerful of which is that common denominator - the "you factor." I can't control or guarantee that you're going to work this system effectively. I can't guarantee that your state, or your area within that state will support the same results I get. I can't guarantee that closing agents, or any customers for that matter, are going to like you and want to work with you. Those things are out of my control. Some of them are even out of your control. All you can do is the best you can with what you've got.

Embrace the idea of constant, continuous improvement. Know that this business is about way more than just knowing how to sign, date, and stamp a piece of paper. This business is about people and relationships. You may have to grow and learn more about yourself and other people than you will ever have to know about documents and ink.

ADAPTABILITY AND RESOURCEFULNESS

Throughout the book, you'll see "Macgyver Notary Tips" that were designed to give you insight into some of the lessons I learned throughout the years. Also, this highlights the importance of resourcefulness. You might remember the old television show, "Macgyver." He was a former operative that could get himself out of just about anything with a stick of gum and a paperclip. The most successful notaries are self-reliant notaries who know how to find information when they need it. Resources can be people, mentors, colleagues, publications, associations, state statutes, the internet, books, and more. Claim your business and your responsibility in its success!

FIND THE BILL EMOJI
FOR THE MACGYVER NOTARY TIPS

A BASIC OVERVIEW

I am a "big picture" thinker. I like to have an idea where a book is going before I dive in to the nitty gritty details. For that reason, I wanted to give you this basic overview of what a Notary Public is, how that differs from a loan signing agent, and the essentials of how you'll get clients and get paid.

INDUSTRY OVERVIEW

WHAT IS A NOTARY PUBLIC?

According to the National Notary Association, "A **Notary Public** is an official of integrity appointed by state government —typically by the Secretary of State — to serve the **public** as an impartial witness in performing a variety of official fraud-deterrent acts related to the signing of important documents."

Depending on who you ask, notaries have been around since ancient Rome, documenting and writing important information, as well as witnessing signatures for important documents. In today's modern society, the Notary Public's primary responsibility is to validate the identification of individuals who sign important documents. The notary can also assess whether or not the signer of documents is under any type of obvious duress such as direct threat, drugs, or alcohol. In this way, a notary plays a critical role in the prevention of identity theft.

Notaries are typically commissioned and regulated by the individual states, namely, their Secretary of State. This can vary a little bit across the nation, but regardless, the Secretary of State is a good starting point for you. It's important to note that there is no true Federal level of regulation for notaries. In fact, thanks to the National Notary Association, and a few other societies and organizations, we are heavily self-regulated in that regard. And since there is no Federal oversight, these organizations have created standards of practice to help guide notaries and signing agents. The goal, of course, is to maintain the integrity of both the individual notary *and* the profession itself. This system only works if we, the Notary Public, fulfill our duty with integrity and competency.

WHAT IS A LOAN SIGNING AGENT?

A loan signing agent is a specially trained Notary Public who helps facilitate loan document signings for the mortgage industry. Yep, that's it. The word, "Signing Agent" conjures up visions of men in black with special badges, but in reality, it's nothing like that. Being based in the hot climate of Phoenix,

Arizona, I rarely wear black anymore. And, I'm still working on special badges.

Signing agents typically represent the Escrow Officer, or Closing Agent, in a real estate transaction. These transactions usually include home refinancing and home purchases. A signing agent will meet the signers at a location to:

- Confirm Identity of the signers.
- Witness signatures.
- Briefly describe each document.
- Make sure each document of the loan package has been signed, dated, and initialed correctly.
- Facilitate the return of documents.

WHERE DO LOAN SIGNINGS COME FROM?

Here's the flow of a typical real estate transaction for both a purchase and a refinance (the two most common loan signings you'll do):

HOME PURCHASE-

- Real Estate Agent (usually) and Home Buyer – Any home buyer can choose a licensed real estate agent to represent them in a home purchase (sellers too, but that's a different transaction). A good real estate agent can help a homebuyer navigate the purchase transaction, negotiate contracts, and have a solid referral network to help the deal run smoothly.
- Get pre-qualified with a lender (know how much they can afford). This is usually done with a loan application and some preliminary information from the borrower/buyer. Signing Agents are often used for this application process too.
- Go home shopping.
- Make an Offer.
- Offer Accepted.
- Contract.
- Open Escrow.
- Closing Agent/Title/Escrow/Attorney- Responsible for closing the transaction and making sure documents are signed correctly. These are the people who hire signing agents to represent them at loan document signings.

- Mortgage Process (This is where a refinance would also begin with a lender/loan officer).
- Sign final loan documents- This is where you come in!
- Signed documents are returned to closing agent for review.
- Final signed documents sent to lender for funding authorization and/or final underwriting.
- Final walk through for clients (if applicable).
- Get keys.

(Please note, this is a very general overview and there are lots of other steps & roles involved. Some states vary in this process too, like Wet States vs. Dry States. More on that later)

THE SIGNING PROCESS

Signings can be scheduled in advance or within an hour's notice. Naturally, and prefer a little bit of notice, even if it's just 24 hours. Let's look at a day where I have four signings scheduled.

CONFIRM

Depending on the time of my first signing, I may confirm the appointment the night before. I do a lot of signings at 4 and 5 in the morning, so it's prudent to check-in in the early evening the night before. Other times, I like to confirm 4 or 5 hours ahead of time. This confirmation process helps me build rapport right away, opens-up communication, and allows me and the signer to get on the same page.

In Phase 3, I'll share some examples of how I do my confirmations. Most of my confirmations are done via text message. Once confirmations are out, I'll plan the logistics of the day. I'll look for the best routes, estimate time between signings, and prepare or pick up the documents if needed. Even though I do all this planning, I remain flexible in case things change.

I arrive at my signings at least 15 minutes early, so I am fresh and ready. If I am ever going to be late (which normally doesn't happen), I let the signer know as soon as I know. I've found that people are understanding about this, as long as they have plenty of notice.

I greet the signer, exchange pleasantries, and get to work. Keep in mind that a lot of the people you are signing are getting ready to move, so their furniture may be packed up. Sometimes just finding a stable and secure surface will require your most adept Macgyver skills. I've done signings in parking garages, the back seat of my car, on brick walls, on the trunk of my car, and on top of garbage cans.

Once the signing is complete, I'll check the package for any errors, and leave a copy of the loan document package with the signers. After all this is done, I'm ready to say goodbye to the signer and thank them for their time. In the car, I have a four-part ritual I do after every signing (if applicable to the situation):

1. I check the package for errors again.
2. I upload or securely send the identification documents (Driver's License, etc.) to the Closing Agent. This usually indicates that the signing is complete. If there is a message that needs to be conveyed to the closing agent or lender, this is when I'll send a quick email.
3. Create and send the invoice to the company that hired me (if applicable).
4. Send gratitude card to the signers or the client who hired me (sometimes both).

Once this is done, I'll drop the documents where they need to go or head to the next signing.

CHOOSING A BUSINESS MODEL

We will dive into these more in Phase 4, but I want you to have an introduction to the three different business models you can choose from for your new business.

- **Independent Contractor-** When you work as an independent contractor, you'll register with existing signing companies.
- **Escrow Direct-** In this model, you actually get out there and hustle for new business, build relationships with Escrow Officers, accept orders, and fulfill those orders.
- **The Hybrid Model-**This is the model I have adopted for myself, and it has worked out very well. In this model, I work only with signing companies that have a commitment to win/win and provide enough volume to justify the time and energy needed to complete their signings.

HOW YOU GET PAID AS A MOBILE NOTARY AND SIGNING AGENT

The way you get paid as a mobile notary and loan signing agent will depend on the nature of the relationship you have with your clients and how you set up your business model.

For regular notary work outside of the mortgage loan packages, your clients will likely pay you with cash, check, or credit card (if you have a way to accept them). This payment usually occurs at the time the service is provided.

As a loan signing agent, you are very rarely paid at the time of service. There is usually an invoice and billing period. The business model you choose will have some bearing on this. Here are the four most common ways you can expect to be paid:

1. **From Proceeds**: When working escrow direct, you might be paid right out of the proceeds for the transaction. This means your mobile notary fee is a line item on the settlement statement and funds from the transaction are being used to pay for your services. This is typically the fastest way you'll be paid as a loan signing agent. You'll complete the signing, submit an invoice to the closing agent, and as soon as the loan funds and closes, the closing agent will cut you a check for your fee. It's usually in your mailbox in less than a week.

2. **Corporate Office:** In some escrow direct relationships, you may actually get paid from a corporate office for the signings you do. This is common for "office sits" or contract rates you negotiate with title/escrow companies. Every company is different in their billing policies, so this will vary throughout the industry. I have a client that asks me to send just one invoice per month for all signings I have done, and they pay 30 days later. Another company I work for requires an invoice for, and cuts a check for, each signing, but it comes from their corporate office a couple weeks after the loan closes.

3. **Third Party:** Occasionally, a third party will pay the notary fee. A third party could be a real estate agent, a loan officer, or someone else that would like to offer the convenience of a mobile notary to the signer. This doesn't happen often, but when it does, I work with the escrow officer to get the invoice to the right person for payment. I am set up with credit card payments, and I accept cash and check, so I make it as easy as possible for the payment to be made. I am happy to say that I have rarely been burned by anyone for payment. Still, I much prefer the escrow officer facilitate all payments.

4. **Signing Companies:** If you are signing for existing signing companies, you are subject to their payment policies. Some of the smaller signing companies pay just once per month. The larger companies are starting to pay every two weeks or even weekly. Still, there are some companies that will pay out anywhere from 30-90 days after a signing.

This basic overview probably got your wheels turning. Let's now look at the complete five phase system so you can see where this is going.

HOW TO GET STARTED:
THE 5-PHASE SIGN & THRIVE SYSTEM

"You ask what is the use of classification, arrangement, systemization? I answer you: order and simplification are the first steps toward the mastery of a subject-the actual enemy is the unknown."

—Thomas Mann

THE 5 PHASES TO BECOME A MOBILE NOTARY AND LOAN SIGNING AGENT

PHASE 1- BECOME A NOTARY PUBLIC FOR YOUR STATE

Notaries are regulated on the state (or county) level only, and every state has their own rules and procedures to become a fully commissioned Notary Public. In most cases, the Secretary of State is responsible for the regulation of notaries, but there are some exceptions to this. The American Society of Notaries, as well as the National Notary Association, have excellent directories for you to reference for your first steps to get started. The process of becoming a Notary Public can take anywhere from one day, to a couple of months, depending on your state's requirements.

PHASE 2- SIGNING AGENT CERTIFICATION, CRIMINAL BACKGROUND, AND INSURANCE

I know jumping right into the signing agent certification *before* you actually do any training is counterintuitive, but I have a method to my madness, so bear with me. And, if you still don't feel comfortable with the order of the system, you can jump to Phase 3 first and then come back to Phase 2.

The only signing agent certification you will need to start earning income as a loan signing agent comes from the National Notary Association. Once you have this certificate in hand, you can *technically* start registering with various signing companies as an independent contractor. Still, I would not recommend doing that, because remember, you still have not yet been trained.

PHASE 3- DOCUMENT, ETIQUETTE, AND PROCESSES TRAINING

In Phase 3, we dive deep into all the different loan types, the documents, how the industry works, and more. This is the real meat of the system. To the degree you learn it, own it, and use it, you will determine how smooth and efficient your signings go. When you have smooth and efficient signings, clients, like closing agents and signing companies, will hire you more. Plus, your self-confidence will soar, which makes Phase 4 even easier.

PHASE 4- BUSINESS AND PROFESSIONAL DEVELOPMENT

Phase 4 is all about growing your business. Here, we will discuss the three different business models further. From there, we dive deep into how to build and maintain relationships with escrow officers, connect with signing companies, and learn the additional skills that catapult a signing agent into the 6-figure category. We will also talk a lot about the other skills and character strengths you may want to learn or enhance.

PHASE 5- TOOLS FOR DAY TO DAY BUSINESS MANAGEMENT

This phase is very closely tied to Phase 3 & 4, but we get very specific about the various tools you can use to implement strategies. We will also focus heavily on day-to-day management, like how to invoice, track mileage, report taxes, structure your business, and build a website.

There you have it! A 30,000-foot overview of the 5-Phase Sign & Thrive System that will teach you how to make $100,000 a year or more as a mobile notary and signing agent for the mortgage industry.

NOW LET'S GO IN FOR THE DEEP DIVE...

PHASE 1-
BECOME A NOTARY PUBLIC FOR YOUR STATE

"The secret to getting ahead is getting started."

—Mark Twain

BECOME A NOTARY PUBLIC
FOR YOUR STATE

Earlier, we discussed how the National Notary Association defines a Notary Public: "an official of integrity appointed by state government —typically by the secretary of state — to serve the **public** as an impartial witness in performing a variety of official fraud-deterrent acts related to the signing of important documents."

The key take-away in this definition is "fraud-deterrent acts." That's your number one priority as a Notary Public and a signing agent for the mortgage industry. Your duty is to validate the identity of the person sitting in front of you. Without confirmation of identity, you can't do anything else in the appointment. Once you have established the signer's identity and it matches the name on the documents, you can move Foreword with the rest of your responsibilities as a notary (We'll review more of those details in Phase 3). For now, let's focus on the steps required to become a Notary Public.

HOW TO BECOME A NOTARY PUBLIC

In most states, the Secretary of State's office manages all aspects of the application and approval process. There are some exceptions to this, so you'll have to do some research in your state. However, there are three basic requirements for all fifty states:

1. Must be 18 years old or older.
2. Must be a U.S. Citizen.
3. No felonies (usually).

Here's the typical process for becoming a Notary Public:

RESEARCH REQUIREMENTS

The first thing you want to do is some research on what it means to me a Notary Public, your responsibility, your liability, and your duties, and be sure that it is something you want to take on. Once you are sure of that, you'll want to do a Google search on requirements to become a notary public in your state. Like any internet search, be careful with your results. I recommend you do not purchase anything until you are absolutely clear on the steps you'll take to complete the process. There are many companies out there that have similar names, and they market themselves as being "required" for the certification process. In many cases, this isn't the case. They are just tricking you into buying something you don't need.

As mentioned before, most states regulate their notaries through the Secretary of State's office, so 9 times out of 10, this is where you'll start. Every Secretary of State has a website, and if they are in charge of regulating notaries, there will be a whole section for you to review.

There are two other independent organizations that may help get started. The National Notary Association plays a huge role in establishing a national standard of practice for notaries and signing agents. In fact, they're the group that offers the only certification that you'll need in order to begin as a signing agent. They offer both free and paid training, membership, and phone support for unusual situations you may encounter as a notary.

The second organization that has a plethora of resources available to you is the American Society of Notaries Their website is *packed* with great information and resources, especially the US map that allows you to see the notary requirements for each state by simply clicking the state.

Their websites can be found on the resource page for this book.

APPLICATION PROCESS

Every state is going to require some sort of application process. Some states are more stringent than others. In Arizona, we have a simple one-page application. Some states are 3 or 4 pages long and require an in-depth background check before they'll even let you get your notary stamp. Every state is different, however here are four requirements that seem to be consistent no matter what state you live in.

- Application must be filled out completely and honestly.
- There is a fee to apply (wide range of fees).
- Surety Bond (range of requirements).
- The timeframe can range from almost instant approval, to 6-10 weeks, depending on the state.

NOTARY "COMMISSION"

Once approved, you will be "commissioned" as a Notary Public in your state for a certain "term." In most states, this is a four-year term. You will receive a commission certificate either via mail or email, and most states require you display it in your place of business. Once your term is complete, you will have to go through a renewal process.

SURETY BOND

Many states require a surety bond be in place before they'll even accept your application. This can be a bond amount anywhere from $5,000-$25,000, depending on state requirements. It's important to note here that a bond protects the customer, not you. In your case, this would protect the person whom you are notarizing in the event of an error you might make. A Bond, if ever used because you made an error, has to be paid back to the surety company. This is different from Errors and Omissions (E & O) insurance, which protects you if you make any errors or honest mistake. E & O does not have to be paid back when utilized. We'll dive into this more in Phase 2.

The cost for this surety bond will vary, but to give you an example, in Arizona, the state requirement is a $5,000 bond that costs $25 *for all four years* of a notary commission. It's cheap! A surety bond can be purchased from any surety company, the National Notary Association, and even some mainstream insurance companies.

On a side note, your surety bond may require a notarization. Some states may have notaries on staff at the Secretary of State's office who can handle that for you. But, some of them may not, so you'll want to be prepared for that. This is an excellent opportunity for you to see the notary process in action!

We live in a country with nearly 4.5 million notaries but it can still be a challenge to find one when you need one. See what happens for you:

- Google "Notary Near Me." What happens?
- How many notary websites pop up? What is the quality of their website?
- Do you have to go to them?
- What do they charge?
- How much would it cost if they came to you?
- Do they answer the phone when you call or text?
- What do you like about their digital presence and service levels?
- What could you do different or better?

These are questions you will want to know for your business!

TRAINING

There is no shortage of notary training available, especially if you go online. Depending on your state, training *may* or *may not* be required. You read that correctly- some states do not *require* training as part of the process for becoming a notary public. Considering the liability you take on as a notary, I *highly* recommend you do some training. In fact, over the long term, I encourage you to become an expert on notary roles and laws for your state. Some states provide free or paid training, while others contract their training to other companies that may or may not charge a fee. You'll get all the answers you need on your state's Notary Authority page.

TIMEFRAME

The application process can vary in the length of time it may take from start to finish. In states like Arizona, you can walk in to the Secretary of State's office with your application, pay the processing fee, and the expedite fee (a total of $65), and by the time you drive home, your commission certificate will be in your inbox. And then you have states like California, where you have to apply, pay a fee, schedule a class and pass a test, pass a background check, and wait 3-8 weeks for your commission certificate to come in the mail. Check your state's notary resources for the expected time frame.

NOTARY STAMP/SEAL

Once the approval process is complete and you have received your notary commission certificate, you can order your notary stamp, otherwise known as your "seal." This is *the* most important tool you'll use in your day-to-day operations. Your seal is also very valuable, so keep it close and safe from thieves and perpetrators of fraud at all times. Most states require you to keep your seal locked up when not in use and take it with you anytime you leave a room. If it is ever stolen, your state has protocol in place to resolve it. It is a big deal, often requiring a police report, so please report it immediately.

THE NOTARY RECORD BOOK OR JOURNAL

Some states require that you keep a journal or record book of every notary transaction. It is highly recommended, as a best practice, to keep a journal even if your state does not require it. There are *many* different styles of journal available for purchase. Some states even let you make your own, so you don't have to buy anything.

Most journals will have a line for name, signature, date document signed, type of document, address of signer, and ID information for the signer.

It's important to note that some states require a fingerprint from the signer and some do not. There is a place for this in most journals. Some notaries still require a fingerprint from their signers, even if the state does not require it. This is a personal decision. However, if you ever have a signer who refuses to offer a fingerprint in a state that does not require them, you may still be obligated to complete the transaction. This is another reason why it is critical to get state-specific training at the local level.

NOTARY FEES FOR GENERAL NOTARY WORK

So what kind of fees can you charge for your notary service? It varies by state! And, the fee structure is huge. In some states, you are limited to charging just $1 per signature, and in others, you can charge as much as $15 per signature. Nationally, there is a lobby to boost these fees closer to the $15 mark. However, it may be awhile before this happens because these notary fees have to be approved by each state's legislature (usually).

Most states will allow you to add on travel and mileage, too, so even at $2 a signature, there are ways to make a living just being a notary public. There are still a few states that do not allow this, so again, this is the importance of research and local training.

As you research, stay optimistic in your realism. ALL states have notaries that have found a way to thrive as a mobile notary and loan signing agent.

Also, to add some clarity here, your fees for loan signing appointments are separate from these standard, state-regulated Notary Public fees.

IMPORTANT NOTE ABOUT WHAT A NOTARY DOES *NOT* DO

The general public has some misconceptions about what a notary actually does. This can lead to some interesting conversations and situations. There are many people who think that having a document notarized somehow makes the content of that document true and uncontestable. This is not the case. In most cases, a notary public is in no way responsible for the content of a document. That means that we, as the Notary Public, do *not* swear to the truthfulness of a document (if a jurat), the signer does.

For the most part, a Notary Public cannot prepare legal documents, or fill out paperwork, or offer legal advice of *any* kind. This falls under Unauthorized Practice of Law (UPL) and should be avoided.

Our job is to witness that the document was signed correctly by the person that is supposed to sign it (verify ID and witness). And, we make sure that said person wasn't under any type of obvious duress or impairment when signing. I think it goes without saying that these rules are subject to each state's own statutes, so you need state-specific training to know exactly what your role is.

FAST START STEPS

1. Visit the notary authority website for your state. This is usually the Secretary of State. There is a link to the American Society of Notaries map with links to governing bodies that can help point you in the right direction on the resource page for this book.
2. Download the required application.
3. Get your ducks in a row and purchase the required surety bond in the correct amount (you usually need this in place *before* applying).
4. If you meet the requirements for your state, apply and pay your fee.
5. Once your notary commission certificate is issued, you can order your stamp/seal.
6. Buy a notary record/journal at any office supply store or online.

See Phase 5 for more information on supplies for your notary business.

PHASE 2-
SIGNING AGENT CERTIFICATION

"Everything you have ever wanted is on the other side of fear."

—George Addair

IT'S TIME TO GET CERTIFIED!

I know what you're thinking- Why get the signing agent certification *before* I get the training? I know that doesn't make a lot of sense to people, but I really do have some logic to this.

First, let's clarify a few things. Despite what any course or company may tell you, there is only one certification that you actually need in order to do business as a loan signing agent. That certification is offered through the National Notary Association. Anything else may very well be valuable from an education standpoint, but will <u>not</u> be required for starting your notary business.

I want to take a minute to clarify that I am not discouraging you from taking training courses or learning. Actually, it is quite the contrary. I am an advocate for learning as much as you possibly can about this business and honing your skills to become a professional. In fact, I even price my course, *Sign & Thrive*, at a level that will allow you to invest in other courses, too. I believe you deserve to know all the information you'll need to make the best decision for you.

THE NNA SIGNING AGENT CERTIFICATION

I've mentioned earlier that the National Notary Association brings a tremendous amount of value to the industry, even if you are not a member. They should be your number one resource for questions and support as you build your signing business.

To become a Certified Loan Signing Agent through the National Notary Association, all you have to do is purchase and pass their test with a score of 80% or better. Naturally, they offer a course to help you pass this test at an additional charge, but it is *not* required.

This makes the entry barrier to the industry easy to overcome. This is a double-edged sword. Passing this test doesn't prove much about your knowledge and ability to do this job well. That means you may take the exam and pass it, but you'll still have no clue how to do a signing or build a business. This NNA test focuses mainly on recommendations and best practices, not what you need to succeed. This certification is the standard, and having it is what I call "table stakes" in this loan signing agent "game." If you want to play this game with signing companies, you have to ante up and get this certification, and the included criminal background check.

This is why I advocate for getting your certification as part of Phase 2. It's relatively easy to obtain, and once you have it, you can technically begin receiving signing orders. This makes you an official, Certified Signing Agent who can begin generating income right away. You can now print that on business cards, update social media, and announce your new business to the world. Make no mistake, at this point there is no way you are ready to take a signing because you haven't even been trained yet. But, knowing that you are now able to take signings is a motivator to get through training as soon as possible. You're one step closer!

You also get a one-year profile on "Signing Agent" from the NNA. This is the main database that signing companies and escrow officers around the country will use to find signing agents in a particular zip code. In Phase 4, we will talk more about enhancing your profile there.

There is also some psychological benefit to this, too. Getting your certification is a huge win for you, and it will boost your confidence as you move Foreword in your new endeavor. And, as you'll see later, confidence is key in this business.

HOW TO TAKE THE TEST

The Loan Signing Agent Certification is offered by the National Notary Association (NNA), so to get access to it, visit their website. As I mentioned before, the NNA is an amazing resource for nearly anything you may need in your business. Please note that this site is designed to give you information that is specific to your state. So, the first thing you'll want to do is make sure the right state is selected for you in the upper right-hand corner. Once you select your state, it *should* remember, however it is a good idea to double check this information as you navigate the site.

Click the tab for "Signing Agent," and you will be taken to the splash page for their signing agent program. Here, they will remind you to have your notary commission certificate in hand before you start this certification process. On the right side of the screen, you can select the "Become a Signing Agent" tab, and you will be given two package options.

PACKAGE ONE

The Complete Certification Program includes some value-added items and the NNA's own training program. The cost of this package is about $180, as of this writing. There are some clear benefits to taking the training course offered by the same company that provides the signing agent certification test. There's a good chance the course will cover the exact information that is on the test. I've heard positive feedback on the NNA course. Most concur that it is heavily weighted on regulation and standards of practice that are actually set by the NNA. This is both a positive and a negative because there is so much more to this role and business that is not covered in their course. If it's in your budget, this may be a good fit for you. If this doesn't appeal to you, don't worry; there are plenty of other training options that I'll go over later.

The other major component of this package is the criminal background check. This check is a requirement to become a fully certified loan signing agent. Since you'll be entering people's homes and entrusted with large sums of money to close transactions, this makes total sense. You'll also have to do this every year to stay compliant. The criminal background check is purchased through the NNA but is actually handled by a third-party company and takes about a week to complete.

PACKAGE TWO (RECOMMENDED)

The second package, the "NSA Background Screening Only," is the one I typically recommend the most. It's "Just the Basics." You'll likely get the one-year free listing on SigningAgent.com, access to the certification test, and the criminal background check. The price for this gem, is only $65. But how do you pass the test without the training? Your full training will come later in Phase 3. Right now, our goal is to pass this test and focus on industry best practices, so we can get the certificate and start making some money. The cool thing about this NNA test is, as you launch the test from their training platform, the Code of Conduct, of which the test is based, is accessible. Additionally, there are links to the Code of Conduct under each question for reference.

Visit the resources page for a special coupon code that gives you free shipping on all of your items.

ERRORS & OMISSIONS INSURANCE

Errors and Omissions Insurance is a professional liability insurance that protects individuals (or companies) from mistakes or negligent acts. This differs from the surety bond you have to purchase at the beginning of the notary process. The surety bond protects your customer or signer; Errors and Omissions insurance protects you, the notary, for unintentional mistakes you might make in the course of your work. E & O will help cover your legal defense and damages you may be liable for.

I include Errors & Omissions Insurance (E & O) in Phase 2 for a couple of reasons. First, you have to have E & O insurance in order to perform any type of loan signing, whether you work with signing companies, or directly with escrow companies. Second, you can easily purchase your E & O insurance from the National Notary Association at the time you purchase exam access and the criminal background check. The price is competitive with anywhere else you may find it. If you'd like to shop it around, many recognizable insurance companies like Geico, State Farm, Farmers, and Travelers offer Notary Errors and Omissions Insurance.

The amount of insurance you'll need for your business will vary. Some signing companies only require $25,000 in coverage. Others require up to $100,000 in coverage, and some even require up to $500,000. In most cases, the $25,000 will be enough for you if you plan to only sign for existing signing companies. Those companies have an additional E & O policy of their own that will cover you as a contractor for them. However, if you have any expectation to work directly with a title or escrow company, you might as well upgrade your policy to the $100,000 since that will be the minimum requirement for them. This insurance is relatively easy to upgrade as you need it. So, if you want to start out with the $25,000 policy for the first 3 months of your business and then upgrade as you expand, you can do that. When you buy insurance through the NNA, they even pro rate your premium and apply it to the new higher premium, so you never lose money by upgrading.

Although these prices can vary by state, to give you a rough ballpark of the cost of E & O insurance, the NNA price for a $25,000 policy is about $26 per year (may vary by state). A $100,000 policy will set you back about $104 per year. I don't work for the NNA, so these prices may vary by the time you are reading this. Your state may have an impact on these premiums, too. Luckily, the NNA website is very easy to navigate for a quote.

FAST START CHECKLIST

1. Visit the National Notary Association's website.

2. Purchase Your Signing Agent Package: Recommendation is the second option, "Just the Basics" that includes access to the certification test, the criminal background check, and the one-year SigningAgent.com listing. The price is $65 (as of this writing).

3. You can buy the E & O insurance from the NNA in this same transaction. They allow you to add on up to $100,000 in most states. The premium should be around $104 per year for this policy, or $26 per year for the $25,000 policy. NNA allows you to pay for more than one year, as well.

4. Initiate the criminal background check. Follow the prompts in an email you will receive after purchasing. Start this right away because the whole process can take a week or more.

5. Log in to your new NNA Account on their website and access the test.

6. The test platform will have a study guide that you can review before starting the exam.

7. Pass the test with an 80% or better. This isn't medical school. An 80% is all you need.

In the Sign & Thrive Notary Training Course & Community, we have a preparatory training for this test. When you're ready, you can check it out in Phase Two of the course material.

PHASE 3-
DOCUMENT, ETIQUETTE, AND PROCESSES TRAINING

"Success has to do with deliberate practice. Practice must be focused,
determined, and in an environment where there's feedback."

—Malcolm Gladwell

DOCUMENT, ETIQUETTE, AND PROCESSES TRAINING

Okay, you're certified. You may be thinking, "Oh crap! But how do I do this?" That's where Phase 3 comes in.

Phase 3 is the most technical Phase of the *Sign & Thrive* system. Here, we delve into the mortgage industry and how it affects you and the borrowers.

We'll examine the most critical documents of a loan package and offer you a method to briefly describe each one to the signer. A loan document package can vary between 80 pages and 250 pages, so this is no small task.

The scripts provided for the most critical documents will make your business life much easier. When you know the scripts inside and out, your confidence will increase. When your confidence is increased, and you know you can handle *any* document the lender throws your way, you'll be able to relax a bit in a signing and let your personality shine through. This is when the magic happens! You can connect with the signer and elevate the signer's experience. This will reflect positively on you, the lender, and escrow officer. You'll be a shining representation of them and their services, and your "job security" will be eminent.

This book can't teach all you need to know. You will likely need additional training, or a mentor to help you grasp this information. When it comes to training in this industry, there really is no shortage of options. Every training system will have its value, and some will be better than others. At the end of this section, I'll give you some resources for additional training should you desire to pursue it.

For Phase 3, I have this broken into four sections:

- A Mortgage Industry Overview- This will help give you insight and conversational acuity around the mortgage process.
- Process Before a Signing- These are things that occur before you actually meet with a signer at an appointment.
- Process During a Signing- This is what happens after you "ring the doorbell" at a signing appointment.
- The Process after a Signing Appointment- This is what you do after you shake hands and say farewell.

MORTGAGE INDUSTRY OVERVIEW

HOW MORTGAGES WORK AND WHY PEOPLE GET THEM

This section is written to give you a very light overview of how the mortgage industry works. This is not designed to be fully comprehensive. I recommend you do some independent research, too.

A mortgage is a loan that a bank or mortgage lender provides to someone using a piece of real estate as collateral. The borrower is expected to pay back the loan at a set interest rate and with regular monthly payments, the term of which is usually 10, 15, or 30 years.

The mortgage amortization, or pay off schedule, is heavily weighted to pay back mostly the interest in the first few years of a loan. As the loan matures more of the scheduled payments is applied to the principal until it is eventually paid off.

Mortgages help people leverage their income and assets in order to afford the home, or property, they want.

THE KEY PLAYERS IN THE MORTGAGE PROCESS

I am going to do my best to give you the list of key players in the mortgage process, so these titles and terms will be more familiar to you.

- First, of course, we have the borrower or signer. This is the person who is actually getting the mortgage, otherwise known as the mortgagor.
- In the cases of a home purchase, there may or may not be a real estate agent or two involved in the transaction. Real estate agents represent the interests of their clients in a real estate transaction. Both the buyer and the seller can each have their own agent. In most states, a real estate agent is not required, but most people still use them.
- The lender, or mortgagee, a financial institution, or individual, that is providing the financing.

- The lender is represented by a licensed loan officer, or mortgage originator, who is responsible for taking the application and ordering preliminary information from the borrower.
- The loan officer will work closely with the loan processor(s) at the lender or bank and gather additional information to help prove the credit worthiness of the borrower to the underwriters.
- The lender's underwriting department ultimately decides if a borrower is a solid risk for their bank. Underwriters use the three C's to help determine this qualification- Credit, Capacity to Pay, and Collateral.
- The Closing Agent is a general term that refers to the independent third party responsible for closing a transaction and dispersing the funds. In some states, this is done via a Title/Escrow Company. And in some states, Attorneys are used to close transactions. This will have an effect on you, as a signing agent, so you want to be sure to do your due diligence for your particular state. The Closing Agent, whomever that may be, is ultimately the party that will hire a signing agent (you). If you decide to grow your own business with what is commonly referred to as "Escrow Direct," the closing agent will be your client.
- The Signing Company (also known as a Signing Service or Signing Agency) is a company that goes out and secures relationships with closing agents, and/or lenders. Once the work comes in, these companies farm out the actual signings to independent contractor loan signing agents.
- The Signing Agent (also known as Loan Signing Agent or Notary Signing Agent) is you. A Signing Agent is typically contracted by the Closing Agent or Signing Company to facilitate the signing of the final mortgage loan document package.
- Once the document package has been signed, the Closing Agent will get them back to the lender. The Closing Department is normally responsible for quality control (making sure all documents are signed, dated, and initialed correctly). They will also make sure that all underwriting documentation and support are included in a file to ensure the loan can be sold to investors on the secondary mortgage market. We will dive into the secondary market more a bit later in this section.

TYPES OF MORTGAGES

There are a lot of mortgage loan programs out there. As signing agents, we don't have to know all the details, so I won't go into this too much. Still, it's important to have an idea of what kind of situations you might run into. This way, you'll have a better understanding of what your signer may be going through, and you can tailor your conversation to fit.

First, borrowers can get mortgages on their Primary Residence (Where they live most of the time), their Second Home (Vacation), an Investment Property (Rental Home), Commercial Property (Business), or even vacant land. As a signing agent, the first three are the ones you'll see the most of.

THERE ARE FIVE COMMON REASONS CONSUMERS GET MORTGAGE LOANS:

1. Purchase- When the borrower is using the funds to buy a home, whether it is a resale (existing, older home), or a newly constructed home.
2. Refinance- When a borrower changes the terms of an existing loan, usually to their benefit. Most borrowers refinance to get a lower interest rate, lower payment, debt consolidation, or to get cash for a particular reason.
3. Second Mortgage- This is a loan that gets attached as a second lien on a property and typically uses the home's equity. A second mortgage is very often used for home improvements.
4. Home Equity Line of Credit (HELOC)- A HELOC is also a second mortgage, technically, but works a lot like a credit card. You don't *have* to carry a balance on it, but it is an available line of credit if you ever need it.
5. Reverse Mortgage- This type of loan is usually reserved for borrowers of a certain age (62 and older). It is designed to give seniors some additional cash flow without requiring a monthly payment to repay the loan. These are a niche product, so you won't see too many throughout the year, but you'll want to understand them, at least somewhat, when you do encounter them.

THREE MAIN LOAN TYPES

In your career as a signing agent, you'll see three main loan types.

1. Conventional Loans- These are your standard mortgages, usually reserved for people with good credit, plenty of income, and a good down payment. These loans use the home for collateral and are not

backed or guaranteed by anyone else, including any government institution. If a borrower does not have a full 20% down payment, they will likely be required to pay an additional Private Mortgage Insurance Premium (PMI), which helps protect the lender in the event of a default. The PMI stops once the borrower's home has 20% equity. We will talk more about PMI later in this section.

2. FHA Loans- FHA (Federal Housing Administration) loans are guaranteed by the federal government. Because of this, lenders can offer reasonable terms, low interest rates, and low down payment requirements, which make them a little easier to qualify for. PMI is paid on FHA loans for the entire life of the loan (in most cases).

3. VA Loans- VA (Veterans Administration) loans are reserved for qualified Veterans and are backed or guaranteed by the government. One big difference between these loans and other loans is that VA loans do not typically require the monthly PMI premium. In exchange, the borrower pays a VA funding fee, which can be rolled into the loan.

DIFFERENT LOAN PROGRAMS

Within these three loan types, there are different loan programs available to borrowers. The two main identifiers that will impact a signing agent are Fixed Rate loan products and Adjustable Rate products.

Fixed Rate Mortgage- These loans feature a fixed interest rate that will never change for the life of the loan. These are considered the "safest" loans and are often the most desirable, depending on the borrower's circumstances. Since the economic crash of 2008, this is one of the major points borrowers will confirm with you.

Adjustable Rate Mortgage (A.R.M.)- An adjustable rate mortgage has a fixed rate for a particular time period (1,3,5,7, or 10 years) and then adjusts according to a certain global financial index (like the LIBOR). In exchange for the potential volatility, lenders can often offer a lower initial interest rate. For some borrowers, this fits their short-term or long-term plans. For obvious reasons, this doesn't work for everyone.

DOWN PAYMENT ASSISTANCE PROGRAMS (DPA)

On occasion, you will run into special programs designed to help homebuyers purchase a home. The terms and details vary for each of these programs. As a loan signing agent, you will not need to know, or explain, those various terms. The licensed loan officer or the lender is responsible for explaining the terms.

However, it is helpful to know how some of them work, so you are not blind-sided during a signing.

These DPA programs can exist at the Federal, State, County, or even Municipal (city) level. These programs can often be used in conjunction with many of the loan programs.

Down Payment Assistance can vary in amount, terms, and rules. The funds are usually used for...wait for it...a down payment. But, depending on the program, funds may be used to help with closing costs, too.

THINGS TO LOOK FOR ON DPA FUNDS

DPA funds can either be a grant, meaning these funds are gifted to the borrower (usually with certain terms) or they can be a loan, where there is an expectation that DPA funds be repaid.

If the DPA funds are a grant, there may be special terms that the borrower must adhere to in order to maintain the grant status. This may or may not include having to live in the house for a certain number of years or make on-time payments on the mortgage. To help protect the integrity of the DPA program, lenders often process these terms similar to a second mortgage. This means, there may be a note and a Deed of Trust/Mortgage document to secure a lien against the property. If this is the case, different lenders may have different procedures. Some lenders will require an entirely separate loan document package for the grant. Others will add just a few more pages.

We will go over a few specific scenarios and documents later in this section.

THE MORTGAGE PROCESS

The mortgage process isn't always easy and smooth. Since the crash of 2008, there is a much higher standard of documentation, so your signers have gone through quite an ordeal to get to the signing table. Some transactions run smoother than others, so it's not always some awful experience. Still, I want to give you an idea of the flow of a standard mortgage process, so you can speak to it if necessary.

The Application- This is usually done over the phone, internet, or in-person with a loan officer. The uniform Residential Loan Application is often referred to as the 1003 (ten-oh-three) because it is the Fannie Mae form 1003.

It usually consists of 3-8 pages. As a signing agent, you'll see this form a *lot*, as every loan package will have at least one of them.

During the application process, a borrower will be required to submit certain information that will help the loan processors compile the data for the underwriters. Remember, the underwriter is evaluating risk based on the three C's- Capacity, Credit history, and collateral. So, the borrower is required to provide proof of income (tax returns, bank statements, and paystubs). This is often the most frustrating part of the whole process for borrowers. They will often be required to submit information repeatedly for logical reasons. In other instances, this request for additional information will defy all logic. Even the heads of underwriting departments can't answer questions of the inefficiency of the system. There isn't a whole lot we can do about it and it does no good to complain. The reality is, if a borrower wants the loan, they have to jump through the hoops the lender requires. Lenders are doing the best they can to stay in compliance within a heavily regulated industry with interpretations of laws that differ between all 50 states.

Once the application and necessary documents are submitted to the lender, the file is sent to processing. This is where much of the information on the application, as well as the supporting documentation, is verified. This is where the loan processor will verify employment, request tax transcripts, run a preliminary title report on the collateral property, etc.

Once the processor has a threshold of confirmed data, they will submit the file to underwriting for a preliminary approval. If approved, the underwriter will likely set closing conditions that will have to be met before the loan can be processed. This may include additional income documentation, Letters of Explanation (LOE), pay off requirements, etc. The underwriters may also decline a loan at this point, too. This doesn't mean the borrower does not have options. They may be able to go to a different lender or just a different loan program with the same lender.

Once all the closing conditions are met on an approved loan, the loan can be scheduled to close. This is facilitated through the Closing Agent (Escrow or Attorney), and it is also where you come in, as the signing agent. The day their loan closes is called their Close of Escrow (COE). This may or may not be the same day they sign their documents. Some lenders allow documents to be assigned earlier than the COE. The day the loan closes, or funds, is the day all money swaps hands. The Closing Agent disburses all funds to the interested parties and the loan is closed.

CLOSING FUNDS OR CASH TO CLOSE

Sometimes, whether in a purchase transaction or a refinance (depending on the situation, even a seller transaction), the signer will be expected to bring "Cash to Close." The amount expected can be found on both the Settlement Statement and the Closing Disclosure. This will not be a surprise to the signer.

As the signing agent, you may be responsible for the collection of these funds. Most closing agents will require closing funds in the form of a cashier's check or bank wire. A cashier's check is guaranteed funds. Please note, an Official Check from a credit union may not be the same as a cashier's check from a bank. Some closing agents are fine with either, but I still like to clear an Official Check through the closing agent just to be sure.

There are times a personal check may be used as well. If the amount to close is less than $500, some closing agents will allow the signer to write a personal check. Again, I like to check with the closing agent just to be sure.

Cash is rarely, if not never, acceptable.

For bank wires fraud is on the rise, and fraudsters have come up with all kinds of ways to trick home buyers into wiring their money to incorrect accounts. Because of this, most closing agents do *not* email wire instructions anymore. They will deliver wire instructions to the signer via secure portals or printed versions delivered to you and the documents to be signed.

When a signer wires money from one bank to another, you will want to be aware of "wire cut off times." You don't necessarily have to explain this to anyone, but for your own knowledge, banks have a wire cut off each day, so signers need to wire funds early, especially for same day transactions. Wires are not your responsibility, so don't stress too much about this.

TRID

TRID is an acronym for TILA-RESPA Integrated Disclosure Rule. It is part of the "Know Before You Owe" initiative that came about after the mortgage crisis. Essentially, these rules require a consumer to be disclosed of the terms and costs of their financing ahead of time.

There is still some debate over whether it is working as planned. Seasoned escrow officers and lenders prefer the old way of doing things. However, this is now the law, and I think it makes our jobs, as the loan signing agent, much more enjoyable.

TRID requires that a borrower receive a Closing Disclosure that details the terms of their loan, like interest rate, term, and payment, as well as a line item breakdown of estimated closing costs. It will also highlight the Cash to Close the borrower is expected to bring to the closing table.

This Closing Disclosure is sent electronically three business days *ahead* of the signing appointment, so the consumer can review, ask any questions of their loan officer and closing agent, and then sign the document electronically. It *must* be signed electronically three days prior to the signing appointment, or that signing appointment will have to be rescheduled. In fact, most closing agents will not even book you as the signing agent until this signature has been confirmed and loan documents have been received from the lender.

This makes our job as the loan signing agent much smoother and efficient because the borrower has had a chance to review the most critical components of the loan *and* has had time to discuss those terms with their lender. By the time they get to us, as long as everything still matches, they are ready to sign.

And, to be clear, yes, the borrower will have to sign that Closing Disclosure again with you.

MORTGAGE PAYMENTS

For the borrower, they'll be expected to start making payments on their new mortgage anywhere from 30-60 days after signing the documents. You'll be able to share with them the exact payment date, usually the first of the month, when you show them the Note and the First Payment Letter.

At a minimum, these monthly payments consist of the principal and interest amount. The borrower will receive a full amortization schedule so they can (slowly) watch their principal balance dwindle down after every payment during the full term of their loan.

In addition to the principal and interest payment, there may be some other amounts included in the monthly payment. If real estate property taxes and homeowner's insurance (also known as hazard insurance) is impounded by the lender, you will see these on the payment letter. And, if the borrower is required to pay private mortgage insurance, this will appear on the payment letter, too. More on these later.

ESCROW/IMPOUND ACCOUNT

An Escrow, or Impound Account, is a special account the lender sets up, so they can pay property taxes and homeowner's insurance on the borrower's behalf throughout the year. Sometimes these Impound Accounts are required by the lender, and other times, they are voluntary. Lenders may require an impound account as an added protection of their investment.

The impound amount is added to the monthly principal and interest payment, so the borrowers contribute to their account every single month. The lender will then pay out property taxes and homeowner's insurance premiums as they come due. Any overage in the impound account is typically refunded to the borrower each year. If the impound account is short to cover premiums and property taxes, the lender will make arrangements with the borrower to satisfy the amount.

This usually means an increase in the monthly impound amount. However, the borrower will also have the opportunity to "catch up" their escrow account with one lump sum payment, if they prefer.

PROPERTY TAXES

Every state and county handles their real estate property taxes a little differently. Just know that, like mentioned above, some lenders will require these taxes be impounded and sometimes they will not.

A note about property taxes for newly constructed homes- When people build brand new homes, whether in a subdivision or on 40 acres, there is usually a lull in time before the taxing authority realizes the change. The county is usually responsible for assessing and collecting property taxes, and the difference in tax for a vacant land and a single-family home can be tremendous. In the mortgage industry, this is called a "payment shock." Even with 20 disclosures about it, borrowers are often shocked when their new tax bill arrives. In the Sign & Thrive script I have created for loan closings like this, I show you a couple ways to share this with the borrower. You won't have to get into it too much, but you'll still want to know these situations arise pretty regularly.

HOMEOWNERS/HAZARD INSURANCE

Believe it or not, one of the most common questions I get in a signing is about the difference between homeowner's insurance and hazard insurance. These are the same thing! Some lenders call it Homeowner's Insurance, and some lenders call it Hazard Insurance. This is just one, of the many, nuances that can sometimes create confusion in the process.

One thing that all borrowers should know, and they will likely sign a disclosure about this (with you), is that they can choose any insurance company they want for their homeowner's insurance policy. A lender or builder (or anyone) cannot force them to use a particular insurance company.

PRIVATE MORTGAGE INSURANCE PREMIUM

If a borrower is taking a mortgage loan for more than 80% of the value of the home, which means there is less than 20% equity in the home, the lender will likely require Private Mortgage Insurance (PMI), which can be paid on a monthly basis (most common), in one lump sum, or upfront (upfront mortgage insurance premium). This PMI protects the lender in the event a borrower defaults on their loan.

There are two types of private mortgage insurance- Lender Paid and Borrower Paid.

With Lender Paid Mortgage Insurance, or LPMI, the lender is covering the cost of the private mortgage insurance, which means the premium is not included in the borrower's monthly payments. This means a lower monthly payment for the borrower (usually).

The trade-off for that is usually a higher interest rate. When there is more risk to the lender, or if they cover more upfront fees, the lender compensates with higher interest rates. This difference in interest rate can vary anywhere from 1/8 of a percent on up. The borrower gets to decide if it makes sense to them. If you're thinking that it seems like the borrower may end up paying more for their private mortgage insurance when they do it this way, you are likely correct. Over the life of the loan, that higher interest rate will likely cost more than the private mortgage insurance policy would have cost.

Another consideration to keep in mind is that LPMI can't be canceled once that 20% equity level is reached. The cost is built into the interest rate, so the only way to remove that interest rate bump that is paying for the LPMI is to pay off or refinance the loan.

In contrast, with Borrower Paid Mortgage Insurance, or BPMI, once a borrower is below the 80% threshold, meaning they have 20% equity or more in their home, they can make arrangements with the lender to drop the PMI (this still *may* require a refinance). FHA loans require PMI the entire life of the loan (usually), so a borrower can never drop PMI without refinancing out of the FHA loan. And VA loans do not have to pay PMI. In exchange, veterans pay a VA funding fee, which is close to the same amount an upfront mortgage insurance premium would be.

FLOOD INSURANCE

Flood insurance is also another big topic of conversation. This particular flood insurance is *not* what your standard homeowner's insurance policy would cover for pipes bursting, etc. This is the federal flood insurance facilitated by the Federal Emergency Management Agency (FEMA).

Not every borrower is required to carry this additional flood insurance. This is only required if FEMA has determined the collateral home is in a high-risk flood zone. Then, depending on the level of severity, they will require a federally regulated flood insurance premium that will be added to the monthly bill for the borrower.

These flood zones change all the time, almost every year sometimes. And, flood zones exist *everywhere*, so no matter which state you are working in, you can expect to see flood insurance.

In many cases, the home in question will not be in a flood zone. However, it can sit in a community that participates in the federal flood protection programs. The borrower then has the option to purchase insurance voluntarily, if they want to. All of this is typically disclosed well before the signing, so you won't have to explain much, nor would you want to. Don't create more liability when you don't need to. There are usually 2-4 disclosures about the flood insurance status in a loan package, so it will be pretty clear where they stand.

PAYMENT LETTER

In every loan package, there is the First Payment Letter, so each new borrower will have a clear direction on how to make their first monthly payment. We will go over this more later on when we get to the documents. In the meantime, here is what a payment might look like with all these items added in.

Principal & Interest Payment: $849.50

Hazard Insurance: $25.00

Property Taxes $150

Mortgage Insurance: $167

Flood Insurance: $35

Total Payment: $1,226.50

HOME OWNER'S ASSOCIATION DUES (HOA)

Depending on where in the country you live, you may not know what an HOA is. These are a fairly recent innovation for homeowners living west of the Mississippi. But in recent years, they are growing more popular everywhere.

A Homeowner's Association is usually a group of owners in a particular neighborhood or subdivision that help create and enforce the rules. These Associations are ruled by an elected board that the homeowners in the area have elected.

When a home is within a Planned Unit Development (PUD), there is a usually an HOA to monitor the rules of the neighborhood, as set forth by the CC and R's (Conditions, Covenants, and Restrictions). Part of those rules requires each homeowner to pay their dues, which help maintain the neighborhood. These dues are often payable monthly, quarterly, semi-annually and annually, but are never included in the monthly mortgage payment. They must be paid separately.

THE TRANSFER AND/OR SALE OF MORTGAGES

It's very common for a mortgage lender to sell or transfer their loans to other mortgage lenders. This is called the "Secondary Market." When a loan is sold to another bank, the terms never change for the borrower. In fact, the only impact to the borrower is having to change whom they pay their mortgage payment to each month.

Lenders sell loans for a couple reasons. First, there are many mortgage origination "shops" that specialize in acquiring new borrowers. Their revenue is created in origination fees. Once the loan is originated and funded, these lenders will sell their loans, so they recapture their investment and can continue lending to others.

As the signing agent, this topic comes up a *lot* because you'll likely be the first person to mention to the borrower that their loan may be sold or transferred. In fact, you'll probably have the borrower sign a document or two about just that.

Most borrowers are fine with this. At worst, they may be passionate about one bank or another that they do *not* want the loan transferred to. Unfortunately, there is no way for an individual borrower to request where the loan is sold.

Regardless of how the borrower feels about this mortgage transfer practice, I recommend you keep your opinions to yourself. I mistakenly shared a story with a signer of mine about another borrower that absolutely despised one particular mainstream bank. I could tell he clammed up after that, but I didn't say anything. When we came to the Uniform Residential Loan Application where his employment and income are listed, I could plainly see that he worked at that despised mainstream bank…as a loan officer (insert foot in mouth).

This brings up a good point:

Sometimes, what a customer does *not* say can kill your business. That's why it is best to adopt a policy where you do not opine about anything, especially details of the transaction (or religion and politics or…anything).

I encourage courtesy, professionalism, and open dialogue, so your reputation and respect grows with each and every appointment.

MORTGAGE ENTITIES TO KNOW

There are three major organizations in the mortgage industry that you should know about. You only play a small role in this mortgage process, and it has a huge impact. It's helpful to your credibility if you have at least some general knowledge of these things.

Federal National Mortgage Association (FNMA) and Federal Home Loan Mortgage Corporation (FHLMC)- Otherwise known as Fannie Mae and Freddie Mac, these two organizations are actually publicly traded corporations that bundle and sell home loans as mortgage-backed securities to investors. Because they are the two largest companies that do this, they have a tremendous impact on standards for the industry. Fannie Mae and Freddie Mac both guarantee the loans *they* sell (non-government backed).

Government National Mortgage Association (GNMA)- You may have heard of this organization as Ginny Mae. It is the government-owned corporation responsible for the guarantee of federally-backed loans like FHA and VA. It operates similar to Fannie Mae and Freddie Mac as a bundler and seller of federally-backed loans to investors.

Much of the regulatory "hoops" we talked about are results of the regulation by these three entities.

WHERE DO SIGNINGS COME FROM?

Now that you have an overall view of the mortgage industry and how it will affect you and your signers, let's look at a condensed journey a borrower takes to get to you, the signing agent.

- First, there is the trigger event, like buying a new home or deciding to refinance.
- The Borrower may or may not have a real estate agent.
- The borrower will decide which lender they want to use. This is often based on the suggestion or advice of their real estate agent.
- The loan will process for as long as it takes (usually between 2-6 weeks).
- The lender will choose a closing agent. The consumer or borrower does have the right to make this choice. Most default to whatever the lender advises.
- The closing agent could be an attorney or an escrow officer, depending on your state.
- The closing agent schedules the closing and arranges for a signing agent, if necessary or requested. This is where you come in.
- Complete the signing and deliver/drop off documents.
- The loan closes and funds. Funds are disbursed.
- Official documents/deeds recorded with county.
- For purchases, buyer gets keys.

This process can vary a bit, depending on the state you are in. In the mortgage realm, there are two types of different states: Wet States and Dry States. These definitions pertain to when a transaction is considered closed, when funds are distributed, and when the buyer can take possession.

Here is a brief description of each:

WET STATES-

This is the stricter of the two types of funding. In a Wet Funding state, all of the paperwork and conditions have to be met the day the signers sign all the paperwork. This includes the Cash to Close-all funds have to be received and transferred that day (sometimes a two-day window to close).

These Wet states are primarily east of the Mississippi. This wet funding process originated back when most people who needed loans lived relatively close to one another.

DRY STATES-

As the country expanded to the West, landowners, farmers, and ranchers were *much* more spread out. Bankers in Philadelphia had a hard time signing, paying, closing, and transferring real estate for a farmer in California. That's where the dry funding process originated.

In Dry Funding states, a borrower can sign all the documents for a loan, and the lender can wait to close the transaction after all other conditions and approvals come through. They can research, verify employment and income, and confirm clear title, even after all documents are signed. The signing date can be different than the close of escrow date. There are only 9 dry funding states as of the publication of this book. The rest are wet.

It's important to understand this process because it has a direct impact on your marketing, advertising, and relationship-building efforts. In Phase 4, we will dive very deep into Business and Professional Development, so you can confidently pursue closing agents and signing companies to increase revenue.

PROCESS BEFORE A SIGNING

So, now we have a better understanding of what a borrower is going through and where the signing will come from as a borrower progresses in the mortgage process. Let's see exactly how that could look for the signing agent.

How you receive a signing order will depend on a few things. If you work direct with Escrow Officers, you'll likely work out your own system of convenience for you both. If you work as an independent contractor for existing signing companies, you'll adhere to their system. I'll dive deep into both of these options a lot more in Phase 4. For now, let's look at the point when you are offered a signing.

The following is a timeline of activity, from start to finish. This timeline could be anywhere from less than an hour to over a week, depending on the order and when it is scheduled.

RECEIVE AN OFFER

These offers will either come from your direct Escrow Officer clients or from signing companies that you have registered with. Rarely will you receive one-off orders from people you don't know, although it certainly *can* happen.

One of the perks of being a Certified Loan Signing Agent through the National Notary Association is the free listing you get on their companion site, Signing Agent. This is a database of qualified and background-screened signing agents that Escrow Officers and signing companies *will* use to find contractors (notaries like you & me) for signings.

There are also thousands of signing companies and closing agents/escrow officers across the country. I'll share more about them later on.

You'll receive the signing offer via text or email and sometimes by phone. The initial information is pretty vague, but it will usually tell you the type of signing, the zip code or cross streets of where the signing will take place, time and date of the signing, and the fee they are willing to pay. One note on pay-keep in mind that these will be regular clients that you'll work with, and the two of you will have established rates for most cases. You won't have to negotiate the fee on every signing. This is especially true when you work for a signing company. They have set rates they pay for certain types of signings, and that's it. For special circumstances, you can try negotiating, but for the most part, everyone is already on the same page for signing fees by the time it gets to this point. Of course, there are exceptions to this rule, too, and you may receive one-off orders from out of state signing companies that only need you once. For these situations, you'll have an established rate sheet, which we will get in to later in Phase 3 and in Phase 5.

TYPES OF SIGNINGS

There could be any number of reasons that a lender or title company needs your services, but there are six main types of situational loan "signing" offers you'll get.

1. **Buyer/Purchase-** This is a borrower purchasing a home with a mortgage. The typical mortgage loan package consists of 125-250 pages.
2. **Buyer/Cash-** This is a person buying a new home and paying cash. There is no mortgage, so no federally regulated lender or underwriters are required. This document package can vary but is usually between 20-50 pages.
3. **Seller-** This package of documents is usually between 20-50 pages as well. These are the final papers for a person who is selling a property.
4. **Refinance-** This is one of the most common signing situations you'll have, especially when signing for other signing companies. This is very similar to a "Buyer" loan package and can vary between 125-250 pages, or more. This could also include Reverse-Mortgages.

Also, in this refinance category, you may see second mortgages and Home Equity Lines of Credit (HELOC). These are very similar in disclosures, and some lenders have almost as many documents as a First Mortgage. Some are super small, like 30-50 pages. A typical second mortgage will have a fixed interest rate and will disburse a lump sum at the time of closing. A HELOC is also a second mortgage. It will be recorded as a second lien on the property and can be used more like a credit card, or line of credit. The borrower can draw on it as they need it. They usually pay an adjustable rate of interest on the outstanding balance (if any) *only*.

5. **Reverse Mortgage-** These can be either purchases or refinances. More on this in Appendix A.
6. **Application-** In a loan application signing, you facilitate the signatures required in the beginning stages of the loan process.

Typically, the lender will have already filled out the loan application with the client over the phone. Your job is to make sure they sign in the right places and collect any additional information the lender may need. You see these a lot for reverse mortgages. Applications can vary in size between 10-50 pages. The exception to this application size is reverse mortgages. Some of those applications can still be a couple hundred pages because of all the disclosures.

7. **Single-Documents-** You'll run into these situations occasionally. It usually helps a lender correct a mistake or missing document from a previous loan signing. These documents can vary in length from a single page to around 20 pages.

ACCEPT OR DECLINE OFFER

If you're available and want the signing, let your client know by responding. For some of the larger signing companies, they'll send out a mass text or email to hundreds of signing agents in your area, so just responding with a "yes" may or may not mean you have the signing. You'll want to wait until you get the confirmation from them.

If you can't take the signing, let your client know immediately. Most signing companies, and your direct escrow clients, will want to know why you can't take it. No matter what your reason is for declining, you should always say, "I am booked already."

ASSIGNED ORDER

When the signing company confirms the signing with you, it is officially assigned to you. This can look a lot of different ways. Most of my clients are direct escrow, so we communicate via text and email. Once I say I am available and can take it, they'll confirm by just sending the client contact information and address.

With signing companies, they'll have their own systems, too. Some are more technologically advanced with smartphone apps. This makes the whole process automated and easy. You can accept the signing with a simple push of a button, and you get instant confirmation of your assignment. Others send email confirmations or have various other levels of technology they utilize.

CONFIRM WITH BORROWER

You would think that confirming with the borrower would be a simple, cut-and-dry topic. However, like many things in this business, it can be a little convoluted because the way you confirm, or even whether you confirm or not, depends on each client's policy. Luckily, your clients will be very clear about what they expect from day one, so you can adapt to their policies pretty quickly. I work with one signing company that doesn't want us to ever communicate with the borrower until we knock on the door. I have another client that expects me to confirm and introduce myself as soon as I receive the contact information. You could experience this and a myriad of other policies on confirmation. Everyone has their own reasons for their policy, and the reality is, there isn't a whole lot you can do about it. Most professionals will want you to confirm, and I agree, it is superior customer service to do so.

A typical confirmation serves three purposes:

1. Introduction- This is your first impression and gives you the chance to start building some rapport with the client.
2. Confirms the time, date, and location of the signing.
3. Allows you to advise of ID requirements and, possibly, required "cash to close." This information has likely been conveyed, multiple times, but people still forget.

Keep in mind that your clients may need to confirm even more information ahead of time. When I confirm with most clients, here's what the conversation typically looks like. Keep in mind, part of my style is professional, yet casual, and I let that show through in my communication. You can adapt this and include your personality, too. I start with a text message:

"Hello Mr. and Mrs. Smith, this is Bill, the mobile notary for your loan document signing tomorrow. I am confirming our appointment for 6:00pm at your home on Windmere Street. Does that still look good for you guys?"

"Hi Bill, yes, that works perfectly!"

"Okay, great! Be sure to have a copy of two forms (or one form, depending on lender requirements) of ID for each of you. I look Foreword to meeting you both tomorrow!"

Short and sweet! Occasionally, the borrower may have additional questions, but this is usually the extent of it. Then, the next day, a few hours before the signing:

"Hello again! I am starting to make my way over to you and everything looks on schedule. Are there any special instructions to gain entry to your neighborhood?" If there is a gate code, this is when you'll find out. This is also where they may be prompted to tell you about a common issue with GPS in their neighborhood.

If text doesn't work out, I try email next and I use the same verbiage. If these two written formats don't work, which does happen frequently, I'll pick up the phone and call the signer. If you can't get a hold of anyone, the expectation is still that you show up at the scheduled time. Most signing companies and escrow companies have a system in place to compensate you, if not in full, for a portion of the signing fee, or printing fee, just for showing up when scheduled. When I can't get a hold of a signer, I let my client know so they can attempt to get better contact info to me. That usually works.

There is no rule that says you *have* to text your client as opposed to calling. You can adopt any system that works for you. If you prefer to call first, pick up the phone and call. This is your business!

MACGYVER NOTARY TIP

You have a stack of papers in your hands that contains an enormous amount of information about your signers. If the contact information provided to you does not work, check the documents for alternative information. Nearly every document package contains a loan application and/or a customer contact form.

That said, some closing agents, lenders, or signing companies, have strict rules about how, or if, a client can or should be contacted by you. Be sure to read the specific notary instructions, or instructions, contained in the order that is sent to you.

CHANGING SIGNING DETAILS

Sometimes, you'll have a signer who requests to change something about the signing, like time, date, and location. Check with your client at escrow, or the signing company first because some of them do not allow changes without it being cleared through the lender. Usually, small changes, like the location of a mobile signing, are just fine.

Occasionally, I have a client that gets self-conscious about their home. They will ask if they can meet me at a different location instead. I still give the closing agent a heads up and this rarely causes a problem. If the client wants to change the time of a signing, as long as you have the documents in your hand, this is usually okay. But again, you'll want to clear this through the closing agent, just in case there is something happening behind the scenes that neither you nor the signer are aware of.

And finally, if the client wants to change the date of a signing, this usually cannot be accommodated, unless it is an emergency. Some loan documents are "date-sensitive" and have to be signed on the date scheduled. If a signing or closing date changes, there can be implications with the final numbers. Often times, tax impounds, pre-paid interest, and other financial numbers will have to be recalculated. This could also affect the cash to close in a transaction due to daily accrued interest and other factors. On purchases, there may also be issues with interest rate-locks, as well. In our role, we do not advise on those matters. Any date change requests should be referred to either the lender or the closing agent.

RECEIVING DOCUMENTS

Documents for a loan signing can come in one of four main ways:

1. Docs may be securely emailed to you.
2. Docs may be loaded to a secure portal for you to download.
3. You may pick up documents from a client's office.
4. The borrower/signer may have documents in their possession already.

EMAIL/DOWNLOAD

If documents are emailed to you, or if you download them, you are responsible for printing the documents. You'll likely print two copies of the entire loan package: one for signing and then a borrower's copy for their records. In Phase 5, I offer some suggestions for printers. Your ability to receive documents electronically like this, and print them, is often referred to as being *E-Docs Capable*. You'll see this as a question on signing company applications and registration forms.

When you print documents, you'll typically follow these guidelines:

- Black and white only.
- Single-Sided.
- Both legal and letter size, as per the file. This is why a special printer is recommended!

*Do not adjust document sizes to try and squeeze four documents (or more) onto one page. Yes, this has happened before and is completely unacceptable and will void the signing. Just print the file as you received it.

PICK UP DOCUMENTS

For your local, direct escrow clients, you usually have the option to pick up documents at their office. Personally, I like to do this for a couple reasons. First, it cuts down on printing expenses and errors. These clients let you make borrower copies at the office as well. The second reason I like to pick up documents is because it keeps you in front of your client, allowing you to interact and continue to build your relationship. Sometimes you can grab some coffee or treats to take with you to drop off, so the whole office looks Foreword to your visits.

BORROWER HAS DOCUMENTS

This is pretty rare, but sometimes the lender will actually send the documents directly to the client ahead of time. In these cases, as the signing agent, you just show up and facilitate the signing, and you're done. Usually, you are responsible for document drop off at FedEx, UPS, or an office. For the most part, the closing agent will have included a pre-paid shipping label, so you do not have to pay for shipping.

REVIEW & PREPARE DOCUMENTS

In a perfect transaction, your documents will arrive in plenty of time for print or pick up, so you can take a little time to review and prepare them, if necessary.

As you'll see more further along in Phase 3, these loan packages can come to you in a variety of levels of readiness. Some lenders are meticulous in their attention to detail, so every line is complete, every box is checked, and your notary blocks are pre-filled and ready for your attention. Other lenders and closing agents leave something to be desired in their completion practices. Specifically, they leave the notary block information wide open to be filled in by you, the notary signing agent.

I've adopted a policy to ensure smooth and efficient signings for the customer. I do all I can to prepare these documents ahead of time, so our time together is optimized, and maybe even a little fun. This also keeps awkward silences to a minimum and allows me to focus on building a rapport with the customer. This leaves a lasting impression on them for the lender, builder, or closing agent, they have been working with.

If you're brand new to the industry, and have never seen a notary acknowledgement or jurat, don't worry. You'll see plenty in any subsequent training you may receive. Plus, you can download a complete practice package on the resource page for this book.

To prepare your loan document packages, you must know what you are allowed to fill out in advance, and what you cannot. Some states are pretty specific about this, and others are not. For the most part, you can pre-fill anything that requires printing (not signing). This can be things like Non-signature line dates, borrower names, page numbers, lot numbers, etc.

Typical items that cannot be done in advance are signatures & notary stamps. In most states, a notary is acting as a witness to the signer's signature and must notarize that signature (stamp and sign) in front of the signer.

MACGYVER NOTARY TIP

If you decide to pick up documents from your closing agent client, it is a best practice to NOT pre-fill ANY of this information. These should be considered originals, and if you make an error or if the details change suddenly, replacing these documents can be a significant hassle for your closing agent. Some lenders have secure portals that only allow documents to be accessed and printed once by the closing agent.

On the other hand, if you receive documents electronically, you can easily print out additional sets as needed. Or, if there is a change, the closing agent will just resend to you for re-printing-no issue

---

More important than even preparing the documents is to review the loan package and get somewhat familiar with it. I like to look at each document and see if there is something that looks odd or unfamiliar. I know when you're just starting out everything looks odd and unfamiliar. But as you gain experience, certain things will jump out at you. By reviewing in advance, I give myself time to call the closing agent or lender for any clarification I may need or to bring an error to their attention. Again, you won't always have time to do this, so you'll eventually get yourself to the point where it doesn't matter how much time you have before a signing. You can just jump in and complete it. Still, this document review is a "Best Practice" that will help ensure smooth and efficient signings.

If you come across anything unusual, or if you have a question about a document, you have plenty of resources at your disposal. Here is the order you can consider. Always remember that certain signing companies and/or closing agents have their own protocol in place, and you should follow that, if possible.

If a *signer* has a question on the terms of their loan, or anything else about their transaction, it is not your responsibility to know the answer. Your responsibility is to be the conduit of communication and put them in touch with the person that can answer their question (usually the closing agent or their loan officer/lender).

One of the beautiful aspects of this role, as a mobile notary and loan signing agent, is the transparency and impartiality of what we do. We do not have to hide anything or anyone. We have no vested interest in whether that loan closes or not, so we should not entice people to do *anything*.

RESOURCES FOR QUESTIONS ABOUT A LOAN FILE OR DOCUMENT

1. Mentor/Coach
2. Secretary of State (For Notarization questions)
3. National Notary Association (for notarization questions)
4. Signing Company Rep/Support
5. Closing Agent/Escrow Officer/Attorney's Office
6. Lender Rep
7. Online Notary Forum (Please be discerning when you choose your groups)

LOGISTICS FOR A SIGNING

First and foremost, it is imperative that you show up to your signing appointments on-time. This is professional and keeps you in integrity with the signer. Remember, you are also representing other people here, so when you are late, it can reflect negatively on your actual clients-the closing agent and lender. You won't fare well in this business if you are constantly late to appointments.

That being said, there are plenty of ways to mitigate tardiness. Any number of things can happen that will cause you to be late to a signing appointment:

traffic, slow signers in previous appointments, late documents, and many more. People are generally pretty cool. They know "stuff" happens all the time. That's why it is so important to communicate with them.

While there are always unavoidable delays, like traffic accidents and road closures, there are still other considerations to always keep in mind when planning the logistics of your signing. Things like time of day make a huge difference, especially in large cities. A signing that requires you to cross town in rush hour will take longer than a midday signing or late signing.

Be sure to build in a time-cushion between signings to allow for unforeseen delays.

It is far better to be early to an area. But, not too early to an appointment-that's annoying. If you have to burn a few minutes, that's better than being late.

I generally arrive at a client's neighborhood 15-30 minutes early. I never park in front of a signer's home when I am there that early. I'll park down the street, at a park, or at a coffee shop nearby.

As a side note, the last week of the month is usually the busiest for loan signing agents. All of these suggestions can go right out the window when you're squeezing 12 of these signings into one day. Remember the essentials of courtesy and respect. Just because we are busy doesn't mean the client is. They still expect you on time and professional.

WHEN YOU'RE LATE, COMMUNICATE!

If you're ever going to be late to an appointment, communicate with those affected right away. With today's GPS technology, you usually have a pretty good idea of when you'll arrive at a destination. As soon as *you* know you'll be late, let *them* know you'll be late. Most people are pretty cool and understand when things come up.

Avoid waiting to the last minute, like 5 minutes before the scheduled appointment time, to give people a heads up that you're running 30 minutes behind schedule. This will upset people. I drive this point home because this is one of the most common complaints that Escrow Officers hear about their signing agents. Many do not respect the business, or their signers, and do not properly communicate. You can build a niche for yourself just by being the on-time guy/gal who communicates.

MACGYVER NOTARY TIP

Utilize your GPS *even* when you know where you are going. While GPS certainly has its limitations, programs like Waze and Google Maps will update you to traffic delays and can give you a terrifyingly accurate Estimated Time of Arrival (ETA), which helps when you need to communicate. If you have appointments around rush hour, or if there are traffic delays, you can click the route options feature, and choose "avoid highways." This will show you surface streets that may get you to your destination faster.

If you are in tune with your environment, you can almost sense the kind of day you're going to have. I can tell by traffic patterns, or initial client visits, how the day may progress from a time perspective.

It's weird how it works, but there are days when *all* of your signers will run late. And there are days when your signers are all at home, waiting for you to get there. There are days when traffic lanes part like the Red Sea for you, and other days when you'll face endless gridlock. Or, sometimes, there are days when everyone seems to be an engineer and wants to read more of the documents than most other human beings will ever read.

If I get the sense, even at 10:00am, that I am going to be running late for appointments later in the afternoon or evening, I send proactive communication, usually via text. Keep in mind, this is coming after I have already established communication by confirming the appointment, so I have rapport.

"Hi Judy and Bill, I am already on the road for my appointments of the day, and a few of my appointments are already running a little behind and this may affect my schedule later. There is a chance I could run 30-45 minutes later than our scheduled appointment. Do you have flexibility in your schedule to allow for that today? If not, no worries at all and we will make the original time work!"

I've only had one person tell me she couldn't meet later because she was leaving town for a month, immediately after the signing appointment. I made it work.

The others are *super cool.* I think that is one thing you will find in this business; you will meet the nicest and most interesting people every day.

And, when you are this proactive, giving plenty of notice so they can feed their kids, go to the gym, work later, or whatever, people don't mind when you run late. It's the last-minute notice, when they know that you knew you were going to be late an hour ago but didn't say anything, that's when things get…awkward.

This can work the other way around, too. If you are running ahead of schedule, you can check to see if it is beneficial to your signer to meet earlier. Sometimes this works even better than the scheduled appointment time for your signer and sometimes it doesn't.

Use verbiage that does not create a sense of obligation to make the earlier time work better.

"Hi Judy and Bill, with a client reschedule, I am now available to you even earlier than our scheduled appointment time. I could be there as early as 3pm, if that works out for you guys. If not, absolutely no worries! I will set up at the Starbucks at 99th Ave. I have plenty of work to do! Please let me know what works out best for you two."

A NOTE ON NEW SUBDIVISIONS & COMMUNITIES

As you build your business, you may work with title companies that handle lots of new home construction in communities or developments that are brand new. This means that Google Maps and other GPS mapping technologies may not be aware of their existence. That can make navigation a challenge. Many people think ahead and are aware of this, offering you detailed driving instructions when they confirm the order with you. But it often slips the mind of busy escrow officers.

Many times, you will not have any advanced notice of this, as GPS will just take you on a route and just stop in the middle of a street somewhere. That's why it is important to have contact information for your signers. You'll also want to build in a little time cushion for your signings, if at all possible.

WHERE TO PARK

A lot of people say I over-think where we should park our cars during signing appointments. I disagree, and by following a few basic rules, I've been able to build strong bonds with signers who may have otherwise been a little cranky.

The general rule of thumb here is, do not park in a person's driveway, even if it means you may have to walk a bit. There are three main reasons for this. From a psychological perspective, the driveway is the beginning of a person's "territory." So, the instant there is an "invader," many people put their walls up and consider this an intrusion right from the start. Plus, you may be blocking another resident from coming and going during the hour you will likely be in the house. Lastly, your car, regardless of its age and quality, may leak something like oil. That can be a pretty big deal to people, especially if they live in a neighborhood regulated by an HOA (Homeowner's Association) that subjects them to fines and cleaning orders.

WHAT TO WEAR

As a mobile notary and loan signing agent, you'll want to adhere to the dress code of the people who hire you. Usually, signing companies have this spelled out pretty well. As a professional, I would leave no room for question on this. If you work with escrow officers or attorneys directly, they may or may not have a dress code. However, there is an expectation that you will always be dressed professionally. Different regions of the country have their own definition for this, so to be safe, dress in business/professional (suit/pant suit) or business/casual attire (slacks and polo, skirt/dress). You never know who is sitting across the table from you, so think of every signing appointment like an interview. Dress to impress, yet also make people feel comfortable. You are representing the closing agent (escrow officer or attorney). Honor that.

As the owner of a signing company, I can tell you that some signing agents take a lot of liberty with their dress. For example, stretch pants, or yoga pants, are not acceptable. Jeans with holes are not acceptable. I am not a fan of jeans at all in an office, but some offices allow it, so use your best judgement.

One of my escrow clients allows their employees to wear jeans on certain days, or even the last week of the month, when it is crazy busy. They are kind enough to extend that courtesy to me and my team as well. Still, I don't take advantage of that. I don't ever wear jeans to work, and I encourage my team to resist the urge, too. As mobile notaries, we already get the luxury of a flexible schedule; we don't need a "casual Friday."

This also plays into big picture thinking. Every signing is a chance to build a relationship with someone that could change *everything* for your life and business. It could be your next client in this business, or it could be your next client for your next business.

You may consider having an extra shirt or top to keep in the car for quick-changes. I am notorious for wearing more of my food than I eat and still have not learned this lesson. I've learned to incorporate spills and stains into my introduction and rapport.

PERSONAL HYGIENE

There could be a lot to talk about in the hygiene section. This isn't a health class, so I won't go over everything. There are some components of hygiene that stand out in our business. Remember you are a representative of the closing agent. This could be an escrow officer or an attorney. Represent them well.

- Smile. This does more for you than it does for your client.
- Be clean.
- Be aware of your breath and do something about odor if you get it. I have stock in breath mints. Days are long sometimes.
- Be aware of dental concerns and do your best to either conceal or fix missing or rotten teeth.
- Make sure your fingernails are at least clean, if not manicured. You will be pointing a lot and they will see your fingers.
- If you have exceptionally dry skin, you should take care of yourself as your doctor suggests. At the very least, cover it up.
- Wear little to no perfumes and cologne. Some people are incredibly sensitive to smell, and others have mild to severe allergies.
- Keep your hair professionally groomed and cut.
- If you have facial hair, keep it clean, trimmed and groomed. Use beard oils for longer beards, and always double-check for food debris in your beard.
- Please, please, please check a mirror before you walk up to someone's home. Many things can be overcome with humor, but you can't laugh at what you can't see. And people do *not* always tell you when you've got cheese stuck in your beard or spinach in your teeth. Trust me…

On the flip side of this, there is no way to control the hygiene of your signers or the hygiene of their kids and pets. Be prepared for everything.

Having some Sani-wipes handy, even if just in your car, is recommended.

RESTING BITCH FACE (RBF)

RBF kills more business relationships than we'll ever know. Whether we like it or not, people are judging each other based on all kinds of information that our brain processes through our individual filters and experiences.

Our facial expressions send signals that are not always, maybe even rarely, accurate. So, when people see our facial expressions, they might perceive that we are behaving or thinking a certain way that is either completely different, in our own little world, or perfectly accurate. Perception is reality.

What is resting Bitch Face?

Said simply, RBF is just the natural resting position of your facial muscles when you are not actively smiling or frowning. Just your natural facial expression. For some, this RBF is actually a joyful, happy look (you know the type).

For others, the natural resting position of their facial muscles just happen to look like someone who is angry, fed up with life (they "can't even"), judgmental, or even condescending. Believe it or not, contempt is actually the most common perception of resting bitch face.

This is a real thing!

In fact, there are several celebrities that are almost just as famous for their RBF as they are for their talents.

By being the way I am, I had to nerd out on this, too, and I found us an expert on Resting Bitch Face. Yeah, there is one.

I invited Jason Rogers, a researcher on facial expressions and body language, to deliver a one-hour training webinar for Notary Coach. If you're a nerd like me, I think you'll find it fascinating. And even if it is not incredibly fascinating to you, it can bring a new awareness to how you might be showing up to the world. You can watch it on the resource page for this book.

While sitting in my car, just before a signing, I take 10 deep breaths, nice and slow (don't hyperventilate!). As I am taking each breath and releasing it, I think of three words that describe how I want to "show up" for this next appointment. This prepares my mindset and energy, so I can be of maximum service to my signers and clients. It creates the signing space.

The three words that come to me the most are: Authentic, Connected, and Joyful.

Yours might be different, especially in the beginning: Knowledgeable, Detailed, Confident, or Competent, Confident, and Likeable. You get to pick!

As I am walking up to the door, I am remembering two things: the signer's first names and my three words. I recite them over and over until I ring that doorbell.

PROCESSES DURING A SIGNING

Once inside, you'll likely exchange pleasantries, greet the family or fur babies, and make your way (hopefully) toward some type of table. Remember what I mentioned earlier: many of the people you'll be signing are in some form of transition, so tables may not be readily available. I'll just ask the question, "Where would you like to set up today?"

Some signers really have no clue how much paperwork is involved, so they'll assume they just have to sign a couple sheets of paper, and you'll be on your way. If that's their expectation, they may offer a coffee table, or a tailgate, as a signing location. It's totally okay to suggest a table because of the volume of paperwork. They'll want to be comfortable, and so will you. I always suggest a dining table, if it is an option.

**MACGYVER
NOTARY TIP**

Some notaries carry folding tables and chairs in the trunk of their car for those occasions when the borrower or signing location does not have one available.

GREETING

Once you ring the doorbell, or knock on the door, prepare for your greeting. I like to take a quick peek, one more time, at the documents, so the signer's name is fresh in my mind. That way, I can properly greet them when they answer the door. Depending on the organization you learn from, they may expect you to show your ID or a business card upon greeting. Because of the amount of contact I have had with the signer by this point, I rarely do that. In all my years of experience, I've never had anyone even ask for my ID. That being said, I'll leave a business card at nearly every signing. And, of course, you want to follow the policy set forth by the person who hired you, or your state's legislature or Secretary of State.

Your level of formality in your greeting is up to you. I recommend you be authentic and natural. Be you!

For me, by the time I ring their doorbell, I have some kind of rapport with the signer, and I am comfortable addressing them by their first name. Most people are fine with that, and if they are not, you will know by the way they introduce themselves.

If I reach my hand out and say, "Good Morning, I am Bill, the Notary," and she extends her hand and says, "Hello, I am Dr. Smith," then I'll call her "Dr. Smith." Calling her anything other than the name she introduced herself as would be considered disrespectful.

CHOOSING A SEAT

Where you sit matters. First, and foremost, having yourself and the borrowers sit in the proper order or place will help the signing run efficiently. You typically want them to sit in the order they are signing, so things flow well. This can shave minutes off a signing and help keep your flow, so you can minimize errors, keep you focused, and give you peace of mind. Choosing the right seat can also be a sub-conscious power submission, so you get less resistance during a signing. People like to feel like they're in control. Let them have that, and your signings will be a piece of cake.

The general rule is do not sit at the head of the table. Many people offer it to you because you are the guest. Instead, let the Primary (first) signer have the head of the table. The second signer (or co-borrower) can then have the next seat on the side. You'll sit across from that person, so the two of you are flanking the primary. When you sit in this position, you can easily slide the paperwork between the two across the table, and the Primary can sign, date, and initial, while easily sliding the form next door to the co-borrower. Then the co-borrower just quickly slides it across the table to you, like a little assembly line circle.

This is great when it works, like on square tables. But, as you'll soon see, this won't always be an option. Do the best you can with what you've got. And, again, don't be afraid to take control here and guide the seating process. This will serve you when you have four to six signers for a loan. Put them in the proper order for signing!

My friend, and fellow notary trainer, Carol Ray (Founder of Notary2Pro) calls this "gentle control." Most signers, because they are unfamiliar with the process and may be a little insecure with a stranger in their home, will appreciate your level of professionalism and thoughtfulness when you take control and show them how to do it.

EXAMPLES OF SIGNING LOCATIONS I HAVE HAD

- Breakfast Bar
- Coffee Table
- Boxes
- Crates and a clipboard
- Top of a trash can
- Back of my car
- Trunk of my car
- Hood of my car
- On a brick wall
- At a Bus Stop
- At Denny's in-between their bites of Rooty-Tooty Fresh & Fruity
- At the loan officer's place of business
- At the real estate agents home or office
- The supply closet at an Ace Hardware (seriously)
- In an auto-repair garage…on top of a tool box
- In the back of a police car (at an accident scene)
- Outdoor Lunch Area at a Large Company
- In a Warehouse
- Inside a skate park
- At a Bank
- Starbucks (All the time)

HOW TO HANDLE MESSY OR SMELLY HOMES OR LOCATIONS

When I first started out, I just put up with anything I encountered. I thought that was what I was supposed to do, just from a customer service perspective.

Ask any seasoned loan signing agent, and they'll have a few dozen stories about the interesting homes they have visited over the years. We've seen it all: hoarders, the "cat lady," pet pigs, the "dog man," and every signing surface imaginable-clean or otherwise. For every one of these bizarre scenarios, there are one hundred normal, clean and tidy signing locations.

As my relationships with my escrow officer clients grew, I started sharing some of these stories, and they were appalled that I was putting up with it!

I had the right, even the responsibility, to politely and professionally suggest an alternative location if there was anything that may endanger me, or the documents, at a signing. And, if there were too many distractions, like kids, pets, or noise, I could also suggest a different location. I may not be able to force it, but I could certainly state my case and make the suggestion.

This changed my business forever!

I don't run into it often anymore, but I don't hesitate to suggest a coffee shop or restaurant as an alternative if the signing location is just too uncomfortable.

One other lesson I learned is that if a signer hints that they would rather meet around the corner, honor it. There is a reason they don't want people in their house.

When I first started, I would counter their question with a case for mobile notaries and the convenience of coming to your home, and almost force the issue. Trust me…there was a reason they didn't want me there!

ASKING FOR IDENTIFICATION

As we are making our way to the signing area, whatever that may be, I'll ask the borrower if they have their IDs handy. This gives them an opportunity to grab it before they sit down. They may ask you if they need one form or two forms, so it is helpful if you know what they need before the signing. In mortgages, some lenders require a primary identification and a secondary, while other lenders are fine with just one form of ID. Let's talk about the difference.

BECOME AN EXPERT IN YOUR STATE

As I mentioned in the beginning of this book, the responsibility to know what IDs are acceptable in your state, is totally on you as the Notary Public. Lenders and closing agents may work in all 50 states, so they won't know what is legal in your state. They will confirm what may be acceptable for them to close the loan but that may not be legal in your state.

You don't necessarily have to be an expert level-notary to get started, but you should chart a path for expertise. I like to think of it this way. Our role, as a Notary Public, serves a very specific role in fraud prevention. We protect people and transactions as they transfer wealth of all kinds, property, and even life and death decisions. This *is* a big deal

On a business level, we could potentially earn hundreds of thousands of dollars a year…as long as we maintain our commissioned status. Lapses in integrity, which includes knowing what you can and cannot do, can jeopardize our livelihood.

With all of that said, let's take a look at common lender requirements including the Patriot Act. The Patriot Act contains clauses that require lenders to adhere to in order to aid in the prevention of terrorism, money laundering, and mortgage/identity fraud.

PRIMARY FORMS OF ID

In the mortgage industry, and under the Patriot Act, there is a list of Primary Identification sources that a signer, or borrower, can use to satisfy this requirement.

If they have a non-expired state-issued identification card or driver license or a United States Passport, you are golden. 90% of your signers will fall into this category. The other 10% may have a military ID, which works as well.

List of acceptable Primary Forms of ID

- State-issued driver license.
- State-issued identification card.
- U.S. Passport.
- U.S. Military I.D.
- Foreign Passports- This depends on your state-specific statutes and the lender requirements. You must ask the closing agent and check your state's notary handbook for eligibility requirements.

There are four main requirements for an ID to be valid:

1. It must have a picture of the person
2. It must have a physical description of the person
3. In most states, it must have an example of the persons signature
4. It must be government issued (state or country)

Also, as we move further into a digital age, there will be changes, so confirm what works in your state.

SECONDARY FORMS OF ID

If the lender requires two forms of ID, there is a much longer list of these secondary forms of ID available to you. With secondary forms of ID, you need "back up" documentation to further prevent fraud. A secondary form of ID can be just about anything that has the signer's name imprinted on it. Here is a list of examples:

1. Health insurance card

2. Utility bill

3. Costco Card

4. Credit or debit card (be sure not to copy, photograph, or write entire account numbers-last 4 are fine)

As you review the Primary ID, you're checking for a few things:

Number one, you'll want to be sure the ID is not expired. For mortgages, this is usually a requirement. However, some states allow for expired identification, so you want to be sure you are up to speed on the state-specific rules and laws. Even if your state allows expired IDs, you may want to let the closing agent know right away, as the lender may have some rules for this. The Patriot Act is a Federal mandate, so an expired ID may cause an issue in a mortgage situation.

Next, you want to be sure the picture matches the person in front of you. Many people have very old photos of themselves, so they may look younger, thinner, and have more hair in the photos. That's totally fine, but you still want to be confident it's them. You can also check the birthdate and make sure the person sitting in front of you reasonably matches the age range.

I can't stress enough the importance of attending your state's specific notary training, even if it is not required. They spend a lot of time on this type of stuff, and it will serve you immensely. And even if the state does not offer training, studying the state statutes regulating notaries will put you light years ahead. Confirming the identity of your signer properly is your "prime directive" as a mobile notary and loan signing agent. If you can't prove the person in front of you is the person the documents were created for, nothing else matters.

In most cases, you will need to collect a copy of the ID from the signer. The best, and most secure way, is for the signer to provide you a Xerox copy of each. They are typically instructed to do so ahead of time, but many people forget. Lots of people have the ability to make copies at home now, so it is likely worth the time to have the signer do this for you. If they do not have a way to make a copy, you may have some other options. First, check your notary instructions for this contingency. Often times, lenders or title companies will provide a fax number that you can give to the signer, so they can fax it on their own later. As an absolute last resort, you can take a picture of the ID and make arrangements to securely deliver it to the closing agent later. Many closing agents provide secure portals for this. And, for information security, many companies have strict policies against this. Talk to your client or read the notary instructions to learn what they expect.

You are 100% responsible for the privacy and security of the information contained in those documents once you acquire them. Be judicious in your efforts when sending or uploading sensitive information, and always wipe or delete those files when done.

MACGYVER NOTARY TIP

Please do not ever make copies of Military ID's, certain Government ID's, or Common Access Cards (CAC's). According to Title 18, U.S. Code Part I, Chapter 33, Section 701, and this is punishable by fine and imprisonment. If these are presented as a Primary Form of ID, you can still add the information from the ID to the Patriot Act form, but do not accept or take an image of the ID.

INFORMATION SECURITY

This seems like a good time to talk about our responsibilities on information security. I am sure you can appreciate how big of a deal it is, because one way or another, you are a consumer.

In the financial products industry, there is an act of Congress that regulates information security for just about *any* company that works in finance, even on the peripheral. That includes a mobile notary and loan signing agent.

The Gramm-Leach-Bliley Act of 1999 set forth protocol for protecting what is referred to as a consumer's NPI-Non-Public Information. This could include things like name, address, social security number, income, employment, and more.

As representatives of the closing agent, we are responsible for the protection of this information. That's why we put safeguards in place like:

- Locked and hidden compartments for documents in our vehicles.
- Home/Office based printers.
- Secured or encrypted Email.
- Flash drives instead of email or uploads when possible.

THE NOTARY JOURNAL

In Phase One, I mentioned the Notary Journal. Some states require it, and some do not. However, part of your agreement as a Certified Loan Signing Agent with the National Notary Association is to use one. This is also common sense.

Once I have done a preliminary check on the IDs, I'll say, "I am just going to fill out a few forms about the identification. This usually just takes a few minutes, and then we can jump in, and I'll be out of here within 2 or 3 hours." Pause for laughter. Your signer's eyes will get huge at the prospect of sitting and signing papers for that long. Or if they've been through this before, they just laugh, and make a joke about having lunch or dinner included.

Signings don't take that long. In fact, you'll likely be done in 40 minutes or so (in the beginning allow for an hour or even a bit longer-no rush!). A joke like this just breaks the ice and lightens the mood...usually.

I will follow up with a statement like, "No, it won't take that long! The signing typically takes anywhere from 30-40 minutes, so we won't be long."

As this is going on, I am multi-tasking, filling out the notary journal.

MACGYVER NOTARY TIP	We often meet people on their best days *and* their worst days. While we might see a home sale, purchase, or refinance as a more joyous occasion, that is not always the case. Divorce, death, financial woes, and family discord can trigger these events too. Read your audience! If they aren't in the mood for jokes, or if this is more of a solemn occasion than a celebration, hold back on the jokes, no matter how cheesy. Trust your instinct here. There are other ways to let your personality shine through.

HOW TO FILL OUT THE NOTARY JOURNAL

I know you're probably sick of hearing it, but this is important: Even if your state does not require the notary journal, you should do it. In fact, I am even going to go so far as to tell you that it would be foolish not to do so. Your journal is a place to document the type of ID you used to confirm identity, the type of document, the date of the transaction, maybe even a thumbprint (required in some states), a sample of the signer's signature, and a place for notes, in the event something was unusual, or you took extra steps or precautions in your due diligence.

If you ever were to get subpoenaed in a court case, you would have this supporting documentation to help give investigators necessary information to get to the truth and maybe even save your bum.

Without it, it's just your word against theirs.

THE ID LETTER OR NOTARY IDENTIFICATION VERIFICATION FORM

The ID letter can have many different names, depending on the closing agent and/or signing company that hires you. It doesn't matter so much what it is called, they all serve the same purpose. This is a document in which you, the Notary Public, fill out the Primary identification the signer used. This will include basic information like name on ID, issue date of ID, expiration date, type of ID, etc. They may even ask some questions like, "Does the date of birth reasonably match that of the person in front of you?" Or, "Does the name on the documents match the name on the ID?"

Once you fill out the signer's section, there is usually a place for you to fill in more information about you, like your name, address, and phone number. They ask for this in case something comes up in the future and they need to get a hold of you about this file. Sometimes, they'll ask for a sample of your stamp and provide a place for that. Some states are pretty strict about stamping non-notarized documents. If you have any concerns about this, you can stamp the square, strike through it with a single line, and then initial it. This gives the closing agent what they need while keeping you in compliance with state regulations. If you, or the state you are in, feels very strongly against giving a sample stamp on this document, you can just leave the stamp off. No one can force you to break the law and nor do they expect you to do so. Many of these documents, as you'll find, are boiler-plate templates for all states.

THE PATRIOT ACT FORM

In most cases of a mortgage loan, you'll need to fill out the Patriot Act form. This is a document that captures the identification of the signers/borrowers to help aid in the prevention of terrorism, money laundering, and mortgage/identity fraud. This is the form that usually indicates how many forms of ID the lender will require.

There are times when this form is not included. That is usually when the application was taken in a live, in person, interview, as opposed to over the phone or internet. In those cases, a loan officer was already able to verify the identity of the borrower and satisfy the Patriot Act requirements. As the Notary Public, you'll still ask for the primary ID for notarization purposes, but you won't have to fill out a Patriot Act form.

There are quite a few variations of the Patriot Act form, so it is difficult, in a book like this, to show you every variation. There are a few things to note, however.

First, in most cases, you, as the Loan Signing Agent, are expected to sign this document, confirming that you did, in fact, physically review the identification documents. You can never notarize your own signature, so you never stamp this document, unless there is a section for the borrower to add some information or make an attestation or acknowledgement about their identity. In this case, the borrower will sign and then you can notarize their signature, signing your own name, and applying your stamp or seal.

Another thing to take notice of is in some of these Patriot Act forms, the name typed under the signature line may say, "Settlement Agent." In cases involving the confirmation of identity, this is actually *you*. However, on other documents, like "Lender's Closing Instructions," this is *not* you. If the line for "Title" is blank here, you can write in "Signing Agent" or "Notary Signing Agent".

I know this isn't really clear for us, but as you get experience, it does make some sense. In short, if it pertains directly to the role and service you are providing that day, it is probably your signature. If it has to do with the rest of the loan closing responsibilities, it is probably for the Settlement Agent or Closing Agent to sign.

STARTING THE LOAN SIGNING

One of the key elements to having smooth and efficient signings is setting proper expectations with your signers. To help ensure I do this every time, I start every signing the same way:

"Okay, let's dive in. I am an independent notary, and my job is to make sure all of these documents get signed, dated, and initialed correctly, so you close on time/get your keys on time. As we go through the documents, I'll give you a brief overview of what most people find important about them. From there, you set the pace. If you'd like to slow down and read anything, please feel free. If you'd just like to sign-and-go, you can do that, too! There should be no surprises today. I think you've seen most of the numbers via email, anyway. Okay, let's get started!"

DELIVERING AN OATH

In many states, you may be expected to deliver an oath prior to notarizing jurat documents. A jurat usually has language suggesting a person has taken an oath swearing to the truthfulness of a document. So, to stay in compliance with the law, an oath should be given.

Some notaries will do this upon encountering the first jurat document. For me, if compelled to do so, I deliver the oath at the beginning of the signing and tie it in to the paragraph above:

"Okay, let's dive in. I am an independent notary, and my job is to make sure all of these documents get signed, dated, and initialed correctly, so you close on time/get your keys on time. As we go through the documents, I'll give you a brief overview of what most people find important about them. From there, you set the pace. If you'd like to slow down and read anything, please feel free. If you'd just like to sign-and-go, you can do that, too! There should be no surprises today. I think you've seen most of the numbers via email, anyway. There are a few of these documents that are based on information you provided to the lender, and by agreeing to proceed, you do hereby swear and affirm that all information you provided in regards to this loan application and process, were true and accurate to the best of your

knowledge, and that you are signing all of these documents of your own free will. Do you swear or affirm?

Okay, let's get started!"

And yet another caveat. Please be sure that whatever oath you decide to use is in compliance with your state law. The oath process in loan signings is very murky. I've spoken to a few attorneys that work in this field, and when I share this expectation of an oath, they are actually surprised we do it at all. In fact, most escrow officers, who are also Notaries Public, rarely give an oath. I've heard arguments that even by signing the document, with the verbiage attesting to an oath, that this is, in fact, a perceived oath.

I don't know if we will ever know for sure what the law expects in every jurisdiction, so research your area, and do your best to comply. It cannot hurt to include it, anyway, so why not. This is part of staying in integrity with your state law.

Once you give the oath, notate that fact in your journal.

THE LOAN DOCUMENT PACKAGE

Depending on the type of loan signing, the loan document package can have anywhere from 30-300 pages in it, most of which will have to be signed or addressed by the borrower. If I included every single page that normally appears in the package, this book would be a thousand pages. Instead, I am just going to include the most critical documents that you can count on seeing during any purchase or refinance transaction.

If you are more of a visual learner, I have a sample loan package available for download on the resource page.

The best thing I ever did for myself and my business is come up with a script for each one of these documents. This helped me systemize my signings, which freed up brain space, so I could stay present with my signers. When you aren't so focused on documents, and stressing about what they are, you can crack some jokes, have some conversation, and connect with the person sitting across the table from you.

As a new signing agent, it's really easy to give only 20% of your attention to the signers and 80% to the documents. That's our natural tendency because we don't want to miss a signature. We are consumed with the fear of making a mistake. Inside our heads, we are freaking out, so we stare at the paper, the blank lines, completely oblivious to our signers. Meanwhile, they're sitting across the table wondering what the heck is going on. As you can imagine, this is a pretty unpleasant experience for your signers.

One of the beautiful things about the role we play in the mortgage chain is we may be the very last face (maybe even the first face) that the signer will see. The experience we provide can enhance and color the entire process, making the loan officer, real estate agent, and the closing agent look like heroes.

Instead of giving so much of your attention to the paperwork, flip that ratio. Give 80% of your attention to the signers, focusing on connection, and building rapport. And the 20% attention you give the paperwork will be your most detailed attention.

When you take time to build rapport and connection, the pressure to perform a perfect signing is relieved. Your signers like you, or at least respect your professionalism. You will have control of the signing. You can slow the pace or pause to read a document, so you have clarity to what it is. With rapport, you can comfortably bring missed signatures, dates, or corrections, to the signer's attention.

MACGYVER NOTARY TIP

As a loan signing agent, our role is <u>not</u> to *explain* any of these documents. Our role is to briefly describe the documents and direct the signer as to the proper way to sign, date, and initial each document. The script and general description you see below is <u>not</u> legal advice to you from me or from you to your client. The signers may, at any time, slow down and read *any* document in its entirety. That is their right to do so, as they are the ones signing the contract.

INITIAL ORDER OF DOCUMENTS

The order in which you start your signing will have a significant impact on how smooth and efficient this goes. Remember, we want the signer to be comfortable and confident in our abilities. So, it's best to start with the documents that are going to address the majority of their questions or concerns. These documents include:

- The Settlement Statement
- The Closing Disclosure

- The Note (Promissory Note)
- The Deed of Trust/Mortgage (and all Riders)

In most cases, your closing agent will agree with you and will send you the documents in the proper order.

Sometimes, they will send over loan documents in an atrocious order. It might make sense for them on the back-end, but if you were to start a loan signing that way, it would make your life much harder than it needs to be.

As we mentioned earlier, the general rule is that the loan documents need to be sent back in the same order you received them. However, in order to provide a smooth and efficient signing, if you need to re-arrange a bit to get these four documents on top, I would encourage you to do so. You can always put them back where the closing agent had them after the signing (use sticky notes or another system to remember what goes where).

Let's look at these four documents more in depth with the script I use to explain them. As we move through this, take note of how important it is that we, as signing agents, do not *over-explain* these documents. Our job is *not* to provide advice, explain, advise, or offer opinions. Our job is to verify ID, provide a brief overview of the documents, and ensure each page gets signed, dated, and initialed correctly. That's it, and it's a beautiful thing!

THE SETTLEMENT STATEMENT

In a purchase transaction, the Settlement Statement is the document your signers will want to see first. It is a line item of any and all closing costs, for both buyer and the seller. For a refinance, if it is included at all, I present it second. The closing agent (escrow officer) is typically responsible for creating the Settlement Statement.

The Settlement Statement is typically two to three pages long and will have a signature page (or two) with it. The borrower is confirming that they had a chance to review the document. In some cases, the Settlement Statement you have at closing won't actually be the final one. Sometimes, there are situations where fees have to be added, closing dates, and interest charges have to be adjusted, etc.

All of this is okay, as the Settlement Statement is not a notarized document. Your signer just signs, acknowledging receipt of the version they have. The closing agent will facilitate the signature of any subsequent versions. Those can usually be done via email, scanning, and mail later on, if necessary.

Here's the script I use when presenting the Settlement Statement:

"Next up (or first up), we have the Settlement Statement. This may look familiar because they typically email this to you ahead of time. This has all the numbers associated with the transaction. As the buyer, your information is over here, on the right.

You can see your contract sales price, credit for the earnest money deposit, credit from the seller toward closing costs (if applicable), and the larger number up here, is the new loan amount.

The rest of this is just a line item of any and all closing costs associated with the transaction. You'll see the lender fees, various title fees, (point out credits from lender, real estate agent, gift funds, grants, etc.). And when it is all said and done, this is the amount they are expecting from you today (This is cash to close-sometimes they owe money, sometimes they get money back, and sometimes, it is a perfect wash and no cash is due, and they get nothing back. Did you bring in a cashier's check for that amount today, or did you wire it already?"

CASH TO CLOSE

This is the perfect opportunity to talk about "Cash to Close." In most mortgage and real estate transactions, there will be either cash due from the buyer/seller or owed to the buyer/seller. As the signing agent, it will be your responsibility to either collect funds due or let the closing agent know what the plan is for receiving that money.

If a borrower owes less than $500, most institutions will accept a personal check or money order. They'll have their own policies for numbers over that, but you can count on the necessity for "guaranteed funds." Anything over $500 will likely have to be by a cashier's check or bank wire. Closing agents usually include some information about methods of payment. If you have any questions, you can reach out to them directly. These checks can be huge. I once had a cashier's check for $790,000 for a home the buyer paid cash for. It's imperative you keep funds secure. Cash is never accepted. Receipts are issued by the closing agent and usually returned with post-closing packages.

If you are accepting a cashier's check from a signer, there are a few things you want to confirm on the check:

1. Check Amount- The dollar amount should match what is listed on the Settlement Statement and/or Closing Disclosure (these two numbers may differ depending on the lender). If the number does not match, ask them why, and document the reason. I recommend notifying the closing agent as well.

2. Made Payable To- In most cases, checks are cut to the closing agent's company. That's what a closing agent is for. Look for misspellings, typos, and accuracy in the name. There are usually specific instructions on who the check is made out to. "Amazon Title" on the check would suffice for "Amazon Title Company."

3. Source of Funds- Verify that the name on the bank account is one of the borrowers in this transaction. This is usually typed on the check. This is also a big deal because lenders have to source the funds from real estate transactions for a variety of reasons. If Robert and Nancy are buying a home, and their down payment check has Aunt Gladys's name on it because she wants to do that as a gift, the lender has to approve that in advance. And, if it has been approved, you'll usually see a note on the Settlement Statement. If not, call the closing agent.

4. Guaranteed Funds- As mentioned above, most closing agents are going to require a cashier's check. Some credit unions use the term "official checks" as their form of guaranteed funds. However, some closing agents take issue with those, so to be safe, you may want to confirm with the closing agent.

If I am collecting funds from the borrower, I usually clip the check to the front of the document package, so the closing agent can see it immediately. If the borrower has wired, or will wire funds, there's nothing you need to do except to communicate that to the closing agent.

In the event the signer or borrower is owed money upon closing, each closing agent will have their own way of handling that. There is usually a document included that will allow the signer to clarify how they would like to receive those funds. This is usually by mailed check or bank wire.

MACGYVER NOTARY TIP

Special Texas Rule! If you happen to be a mobile notary and loan signing agent in the state of Texas, there is a strict law you'll have to adhere to for refinance transactions and Home Equity Lines of Credit (HELOC's) that are classified as "Cash Out." Texas requires that these signings take place at a title/escrow, the lenders office or an attorney's office. These signing appointments still come through the regular channels so you will likely need to know that "Cash Out" in Texas usually means you will be responsible for finding an office space that meets the legal requirement. And, there is usually a fee for use of that office space. You can negotiate the reimbursement of that fee with the hiring company (usually).

CLOSING DISCLOSURE

The Closing Disclosure (often referred to as the CD) is a 5-7 page document. It was introduced in October 2015 as part of TRID and the new transparency policies.

The CD combined and replaced two documents- The Truth in Lending Disclosure and the HUD-1 Settlement Statement. It is created, by the lender in each transaction.

Like the Settlement Statement, the Closing Disclosure includes a detailed line item of any and all closing costs associated with their transaction. In fact, pages 2-4 of the Closing Disclosure contain much of the same line item information as the Settlement Statement. This plays a role in how we present this document.

Where you'll see the difference is that page one of the CD has an overview of the specific loan details like term, interest rate, monthly payment, and Cash to Close.

And page 5 typically has the long-term costs of the loan like Annual Percentage Rate and Total of Monthly Payments over the entire term of the loan. Additionally, on page 5, you'll find the contact information (phone number and email address) to all principal parties to a transaction. This includes:

- The Closing/Settlement Agent

- The Loan Officer/Lender
- The Real Estate Broker (if applicable and both buyer and seller side)
- Mortgage Broker (if applicable)

If a borrower has a question about the terms of their transaction then, you have all the resources to put them in touch with who they need to ask. Be the conduit of communication here. As the loan signing agent, we get the pleasure of having a transparent, neutral role. We don't have to protect anyone from the consumer. No need to jam things up. Let's help them get their questions answered, so we can have a smooth and efficient signing.

By TRID regulations, the borrower *must* be able to review the CD, electronically sign it, and indicate that they have reviewed it at least *three* business days prior to their loan document signing.

As the loan signing agent, you are *not* responsible for managing that, however it does impact you at times during a transaction. I've been rescheduled many times because the closing agent discovers the CD was not signed on the proper date.

As mentioned before, the good news is the borrower has had plenty of time to review all of the closing costs and terms of the loan, long before they sit down with us. That means they've had a chance to ask questions of their loan officer and real estate agent and should be good to go. Notice I said "should…"

There are exceptions to everything, and every now and again, you'll come across a borrower that signed off on the Closing Disclosure but didn't actually review it.

At times, you may have a CD at the signing that differs from the previously disclosed CD, and that may prompt some questions from the borrower.

Remember, it is not your responsibility to know and understand why these are different. You do not have to explain anything. I like to check for anything obvious that may explain the difference, but if I don't immediately see it, I offer to contact the loan officer or closing agent or encourage them to do so. Remember, all that contact info is on page 5 of the CD anyway.

HOW TO BRIEFLY DESCRIBE THE CD

Again, we want to stick to our policy of "Brief Description" when we show this to the borrower. With the strict regulation on disclosure, many lenders have sent out *many* variations and versions of this document throughout the loan process, so the borrower will recognize this one. Let's use that to our advantage.

In a refinance transaction, this is the first of the critical documents that I'll show. I like to start here because it has all the terms of the new loan, which is what most people in a refinance are most concerned with. I then would show the Settlement Statement (if included at all) second.

Here's my script and style on the CD for a fixed interest rate mortgage.

"Next up (or first up, depending on order), we have the Closing Disclosure. This probably looks familiar to you because you had to sign this electronically before we got here. The Closing Disclosure gives an overview of all the loan details. You can see here that you have a _____ (number of years, or term) year_____(conventional, FHA, VA) loan.

Here is your fixed interest rate (note I don't say the actual interest rate). And if we skip down here, this is your new monthly payment, including the property taxes, home-owners/hazard insurance, and the monthly mortgage insurance. (I typically skip the principal and interest only payment section, so I don't get their hopes up with a lower payment. I skip to the next section that shows the principal, interest, taxes, hazard insurance, mortgage insurance, and total payment, if applicable. Please note, there are check boxes indicating whether or not taxes, insurance, or mortgage insurance are included. Adjust the script accordingly)

This does not include HOA dues; you will pay those separately.

Here is a summary of your total closing costs, and here is how much the title company is expecting today, which we've already discussed.

Any questions on this?

Great, we just need to jump over here to page 5 because the rest of this is just a recap of what we went over on the Settlement Statement, and then you'll just sign and date here."

There can be some confusion on how the CD is laid out. If you follow this script, it will help navigate the page and answer questions pre-emptively, allowing for a smooth and efficient signing.

I also modify this a bit if there is an Adjustable Rate Mortgage (ARM).

NOTE OR PROMISSORY NOTE

The Note, often called the Promissory Note is arguably the most important document in the whole stack (to the lender, anyway).

The Note is the borrower's promise to repay the loan.

It will outline most of the loans terms and conditions and is usually somewhere between 2-4 pages in length.

The Note document can look different depending on the lender and the state the property is located in. In some cases, it may require borrower initials on each page, plus a signature from each borrower.

When describing the Note, I focus on a few main points:

- Loan Amount
- Interest Rate
- First Payment Due Date
- Pre-Payment Clause
- Late Fee
- Principal & Interest Only Payment
- "The Rest"

Here's what that sounds like:

"The next document is the Note. This is your promise to repay the loan, so it again, has most of the terms of the loan laid out for you. These numbers will look very similar to what we just went over on the Closing Disclosure.

We have your loan amount (point at each section as I mention it) here, your interest rate (fixed or adjustable), and here is your first payment due date.

You have a right to repay this loan at any time with no pre-payment penalties (This is a big deal for people to know. We don't see pre-payment penalties much anymore, but if there is one, you need to adjust this or just direct them to read the clause).

Each month, you are given a ____(15)____ day grace period, then after day ____16____ they will charge you 4 or 5% of your principal and interest payment (I point back at page one payment amount here) as your late fee.

The rest of this talks about what happens if you just stop making payments altogether. There are some ramifications for that.

Please sign here, and please do not date this one."

Why no date? Lenders are *very* particular about this. Please *only* have the signer date *if* the signature line calls for a date. If it does not, instruct the signer, as per the script, *not* to date it.

The Note is just about the only document that should *never* have any write-ins, corrections or changes. If a mistake is made on the Note, it is best practice to replace the document altogether because this may hold up funding. You can use the Note from the borrower's copies that you bring along with you, or if those are not available, you can ask the borrower if you can print a clean copy using their printer.

Another *huge* thing to take "note" of on the Note: The Note must be dated on or *before* the signing date- *never* after. You can find the date on the front page, usually in the upper left. This date is critical on the Note only, for the most part.

Many other documents will have "draft dates" that will not impact the transaction at all. This date on the Note could invalidate the entire purchase and leave the lender or the title company on the hook.

It's easy to remember this because a person can never sign a document in the future. So, if the Note is dated February 22, but it is only February 21, then technically that document or contract is not yet in existence, so it cannot be signed.

There are safeguards in place to keep this from happening, *but* they still slip through. Make it a habit to check the Note date before *every* signing. You just might end up being the hero that saves a transaction.

A few years ago, one of my notaries signed a loan package without double-checking the Note date. The signing occurred in a title office, so her guard was down, thinking that all would be well, since the documents were literally just created and printed.

When the docs were signed, they were checked by the escrow assistant and approved. Then, they were sent to the lender and approved. After that approval, the documents were sent to the lender's closing department, and approved. Finally, the loan was closed and funded and the homeowner was allowed to move in. The loan was sold on the secondary market and all looked well. Six months later, the "investor", or new lender in this case, audited their files and one person, in this entire chain, caught the fact that the Note was actually dated for the day *after* the signing took place. Deal-breaker. The title company ended up having to buy back the mortgage.

Luckily, because so many levels of the system failed, our company, and my notary, were not held liable, and it did not impact the relationship with my client. They were actually able to restructure and resolve the issue.

ALLONGE TO THE NOTE

Many Notes you come across will have an additional page called an Allonge attached. This is an extension of the Note document that helps future note holders (i.e. other lenders) maintain their rights. There may often be a number of different lenders in the life of the loan. Many mortgage loans are sold repeatedly on the secondary market. Having an Allonge on the Note provides the extra space for the endorsements necessary to make that possible.

There is rarely, if ever, any action required from you or your borrower on the Allonge, even when it looks like there are signature lines. If you read carefully, these signature lines are clearly laid out for a lender, at some point.

If initials have been required on the rest of the Note, you may double-check to see if initials are required on the Allonge. It is rare that they would require this, even if the rest of the document did require initials, but check to be sure.

VA NOTE

When a borrower gets a VA loan, the Note will look a little bit different because there will be some verbiage about how the loan can be assumed. In some cases, a VA mortgage can be assumed or transferred to an equally qualified person. We don't have to get into this much because we cannot offer advice.

I do not adjust my script for this, except to acknowledge that there is verbiage contained regarding the assumption of the mortgage down the road.

NOTE RIDERS

A "Rider" is an additional document that "rides along" a main document, usually offering clarification of terms or some additional terms regarding the transaction.

Under special circumstances, a Note may have one or more Riders.

TRUST RIDER

When a loan is being closed inside the Trust of one or more people, the lender will add a Trust Rider to the Note. This adds some clarity on what is happening and who is still responsible for the repayment of the loan.

DEED OF TRUST OR MORTGAGE

Depending on the state you're in, you'll see either a Mortgage document or a Deed of Trust. Essentially, these documents perform the function of "attaching" the loan to the collateral property.

This is one of the critical documents in a transaction and is recorded with the county to officially show ownership of a property. Because of this, the Deed of Trust or Mortgage documents also typically become a matter of public record. Most of these will also be notarized.

From there, each state will have some differences in language and clauses, and many of them directly impact the borrower. Still, in each state, these documents are pretty much boiler-plate templates, so we can come up with a good general script that can apply to 95% of the signings we encounter as loan signing agents.

I happen to live in a state where we use a Deed of Trust.

Below, you will find the script that I use to briefly describe the elements of the document. Keep in mind that this is *not* a law book. In our capacity as a loan signing agent, we never offer this as legal advice. It's also not designed to be all encompassing. Our job is to provide a brief description of the document. If a signer would like to slow down and read more, we've already set the expectation that they can do that.

The script below helps you communicate with the signer without giving them legal advice. I've showed this script to attorneys and my colleagues in this industry, and they agree it's a good model to follow.

"Next up is called the Deed of Trust/Mortgage. It's one of the most important documents you'll sign today because it goes over all the landowner requirements for the state of_____. It's also one of the longest documents, with _____ pages (numbered at bottom) of fascinating legal jargon. Lucky for us, we do not have to go through line by line, and page by page today. It's mainly a boiler plate template for everyone.

Still, even though we're not going through the whole thing, they recommend you take a look at it at some point because this will go over how people can put liens on your property, your insurance and maintenance requirements. This also goes over exactly what can happen if you were to default on your loan.

This is also recorded with county, making transfer of ownership complete.

The two things I would like to verify today are how you'll hold title. I show it is the two of you, as a married couple (adjust to situation) and as Community Property with Right of Survivorship (adjust to situation).

And, we also want to double check the property address here.

If this all looks correct, I will have you jump over here to page _____ and each sign (and date if applicable). Then, I'll notarize here."

Some lenders do require each page of the Deed of trust/Mortgage to be initialed and this is usually clear by the line and word "initials" in the lower right-hand corner of each page. Each borrower listed on the signature page needs to initial. They will need to use each initial in their name, as printed on the signature line. For instance, if the name is typed William David Smith, the borrower would need to initial as WDS. If the name was just William Smith, then WS would suffice.

Watch out for the tricky initial line on the signature page, as well as the notary acknowledgement page! Even when the borrower signs that page, and when there is a separate acknowledgement page, those are all still part of the Deed Of Trust/Mortgage document and will require initials (if the rest of the pages did).

EXHIBIT A

Exhibit A is included with most Deeds of Trust/Mortgage documents as an add-on document. It will, at some point, contain the legal description of the property. Sometimes that legal description is already typed in there, and sometimes it will be added later.

There is no action required on Exhibit A.

RIDERS TO THE DEED OF TRUST OR MORTGAGE

The Deed of Trust/Mortgage document can have "Riders" in many cases. Remember, riders are documents that "ride along" with the original document and serve to add additional terms and conditions, stipulations, or clarity to a transaction.

As a loan signing agent, you'll see five common types of riders on the Deed of Trust/Mortgage.

PLANNED UNIT DEVELOPMENT RIDER

The Planned Unit Develop Rider, or PUD, is typically applied when a property is in a planned community with a Home Owner's Association.

The PUD outlines the responsibilities of the homeowner to adhere to the rules of the community and much more. It is usually only about two pages.

VA RIDER

The VA Rider rides along the VA loans and stipulates that the loan is guaranteed by Veteran's Affairs and outlines the assumption policies.

CONDOMINIUM RIDER

The Condominium Rider can be similar to the PUD Rider. This merely advises a borrower of the condominium relationship and some details about the community.

TRUST RIDER

If a borrower chooses to close the loan and hold the property in a family trust, there will be a Trust Rider accompanying the Deed of Trust/Mortgage document. This document usually shows the details of the family trust.

1-4 FAMILY RIDER

You'll see this Rider to the Deed of Trust/Mortgage when the subject property is being used as an investment property. As part of the Deed of trust/Mortgage, this is recorded so everyone is aware that this is an investment property. It will contain language advising the owner/borrower that any rents collected by tenants must first be used to satisfy any mortgage payments, property taxes, and homeowners insurance requirements.

LOTS OF OTHER DOCUMENTS

A mortgage loan document package can have hundreds of pages to it. We won't be able to list every possible document you may see in every state, but here are a few additional critical documents to look out for. This list of documents also highlights the importance of additional training resources that I have provided at the end of this phase.

NOTICE OF RIGHT TO CANCEL

Under certain conditions, a borrower may have a Right to Cancel (RTC) or rescind their refinance loan. Some states can have their own rules on this for purchases, although that is pretty rare to see. There may be a "cooling off period" in some states, too.

You will see the RTC mainly in refinance transactions (it is a federal mandate), so it applies to all states. In order for a borrower to have a right to cancel their refinance transaction, three things must be in place:

1. This must be their primary residence (No investment or Second Homes).
2. It must be a refinance or HELOC (Does not apply to purchases).
3. This must be refinanced outside their current lender (If using same lender, no RTC required).

The borrower has until midnight of the third business day after signing their loan signing to cancel. The first business day after the signing is day one (Sundays and certain holidays don't count).

The best resource I've found to help navigate this is the rescission calendar on the NNA's website. Just Google "NNA Rescission Calendar," and their PDF calendar of the whole year will show up. This is will be particularly helpful when you have to make changes to the RTC.

4506 AND 4506-T REQUEST FOR TRANSCRIPT OF TAX RETURN

This is one of the most common, and replicated, forms in the home loan process. Borrowers are asked to sign this multiple times through a transaction. It allows a lender to request the borrower's tax transcripts or tax return information. Lenders do this to confirm income information and adhere to state and federal banking regulations. The request is only valid for 90-120 days, which is why lenders require so many to be signed throughout the process, as well as at the final document signing with you.

UNIFORM RESIDENTIAL LOAN APPLICATION (FORM 1003, SAID, "TEN-OH-THREE")

This is the final typed version of the original loan application that the borrower submitted. This is one of the critical documents in a loan package. The loan app can be anywhere from 3-7 pages (or more) and will require multiple signatures throughout the document.

DPA SCENARIOS AND SILENT SECONDS

A DPA is a loan program with a Down Payment Assistance component. This means the borrower is most likely buying a home they will use as their Primary Residence.

Certain lenders, cities, states, and even counties often have incentives for buying a home in their area. This incentive might be a certain amount of money toward the down payment or closing costs involved in that purchase.

The DPA funds might be as a full grant (no repayment required), a grant with conditions (might have to repay if certain conditions are not met), or a loan.

The paperwork for DPA funds will vary between lenders and the institutions that offer them.

CUSTOMER SATISFACTION SURVEYS

Sometimes, lenders and title companies will include a customer satisfaction survey in the loan package. I usually present these as the very last documents for the signers to address. While they fill this out, I say, "I'll double-check the documents to be sure we did it all correctly." Most signers really appreciate your extra attention to detail.

These customer satisfaction surveys are actually pretty important for your client, the person who hired you to do the signing. Many times, these Escrow Officers, Closing Agents, and Loan origination team members are bonused based on these results. You always want to keep your relationship win-win with them, so help them out, and encourage your signers to fill out the surveys. Of course, if a signer doesn't want to participate, they certainly do not have to, so don't confront people over this.

COMMON TITLE/ESCROW/CLOSING DOCUMENTS

In addition to the lender documents, each closing agent will have a small bundle of documents of their own to include. These are usually pretty standard disclosures that keep a closing agent compliant with their state laws and company policies. You'll likely see:

- Privacy Disclosures
- HOA Disclosures
- Contact Information Forms
- How to Receive Funds Forms
- Key Release Forms (If applicable)

- And any number of others

These are usually just intermixed with the lender documents, so it may not be super obvious where these title docs start and end, especially if you're brand new to the industry. It really makes no difference to us, as loan signing agents, where the docs come from. Our role is to make sure everything gets signed, dated, and initialed correctly.

OTHER SIGNING SITUATIONS

NON-BORROWING SPOUSE

Every state can be a little different when it comes to rules around a Non-Borrowing Spouse. A Non-Borrowing Spouse is simply a spouse of a borrower that is *not* on the loan. This non-borrowing spouse may or may not be on the title to the house, even without being on the loan. That means they may sign the Deed of Trust/Mortgage and some other documents, but not the Note and lending documents.

This is why being present in your signings is so important. You don't want to assume that a spouse is just going to sign everything just because they are a spouse.

It is important to review the documents, get a feel for what the situation is, and then keep your eyes and attention out for who signs what and where.

OVER-SIGNING/UNDER-SIGNING

"Over-Signing", and especially "Under-Signing," are two terms you'll likely hear a lot in your career as a loan signing agent. "Under-Signing" is the act of signing less than the full name expected on a signature. For instance, William David Smith, as it is typed on the document, only signs William Smith or Bill Smith.

That is considered "Under-signing," and *many* lenders will not accept it. The typical exception is when the signature is completely illegible, like with a squiggle signature. In cases where the signature is illegible, *and* matches the signature on the ID they presented, you're likely okay...but not always (Contact the closing agent for clarity).

In cases of "Over-Signing," the borrower prefers to sign William David Smith, even though his name is typed William Smith. This is usually acceptable, as long as the ID matches (He does actually have to be William David Smith).

HOW TO CORRECT A SIGNING OR DATE ERROR

There is a very specific way to correct errors on most documents in a signing.

For the most part, a borrower can correct a mistake by striking through the error with one single line, initialing it, and then making the correction.

The goal is to keep it clean, so only one single line to strike through.

If a signer makes a mistake on an area they are already initialing, this rule is the same. They strike through their mistaken initials. Initial the mistake. Then, initial the correct way they were originally supposed to have initialed. Seems ridiculous, but it is what it is.

There is one universal exception to this correction technique and that is on the Note. Because of the importance of the Note, most lenders want a clean, error free Note.

If one of your signers makes a mistake on the note, rather than strikethrough it, consider replacing the document altogether with the Note in the borrower's copies that you bring to the signing.

MACGYVER NOTARY TIP

When at all possible, have the signer use the exact same pen they had used for the rest of the signing. Differences in ink *can* present a problem with some lenders. This is one of the main reasons I use the same pens *every* time on *every* signing.

POWER OF ATTORNEY SIGNINGS

When a signer will not be physically present at the signing appointment, they may assign an Attorney-in-Fact, designated by a Power of Attorney (POA) document. In many cases, this is a husband or a wife signing for their spouse who may be abroad, in prison, traveling, in the hospital, on the International Space Station, etc.

While this certainly adds time to a signing, you will not have to verify the POA in most states. Both the closing agent and the lender will have facilitated and approved this process and relationship ahead of time.

Whomever is the Attorney-in-Fact will have to sign in a very particular way. And, if they are also the co-borrower on a loan, they will also have to sign for themselves.

Here is a traditional way a AIF will have to sign:

_____

Marc Jacob Smith by Anne Marie Smith, as Attorney in Fact

Yup…every…single…line…

Then, when Anne Marie Smith has to initial for her husband, it will have to look like this:

MJS by AMS as AIF

Yup, every single time Mr. Smith is expected to initial a document, Anne Marie will have to initial like that.

TRUST SIGNINGS

You'll run into Trust signings quite a bit as a loan signing agent. These are no big deal, but there is some nuance to them, and they do require special attention from you.

Let's talk a quick minute on what a trust is. A Trust, or Family Trust, is a legal instrument, an entity really, that helps hold and protect assets.

Anyone can have a trust, and these are not reserved for the "wealthy."

When someone chooses to close their home inside their trust, the lender must first approve it. Then, they'll draft the paperwork appropriately.

Like the POA paperwork, each line the borrower signs has some very specific verbiage underneath. The difference with trust signings is that sometimes the borrower can sign just as they normally would, as an individual. Sometimes the borrower must sign as a trustee, meaning they have to literally sign the word, "trustee," after their name on each line.

Despite what you may hear, there is no standard way to sign these things. The language typed below the line varies, although it seems we are finally moving into some logical standardization. Even with some standardization on the verbiage *below* the line, there is still lots of variance *above* the line.

Here's what you'll likely see typed below each signature line:

"John Smith, both individually, and as Trustee of the John Smith Family Trust dated February 18, 2005."

Unlike the Power of Attorney signing, the borrower does not have to sign that whole line. However, depending on the lender, closing agent, and sometimes even an over-zealous signing company rep, how the borrower signs will vary.

Some lenders require he sign like this:

John Smith, Trustee

Other lenders go the more logical route and have him sign like this:

John Smith

This makes the most sense to me because the legal verbiage under the line already acknowledges that he is signing as *both* individual *and* as trustee. Doesn't that seem logical? Alas, in this business, logic doesn't always prevail.

Even with thousands of signings under my belt, I still ask my closing agent client how the borrower should sign the docs. And guess what- even though my closing agent clients stay the same, the lenders change, and so do the requirements. Sometimes I have to instruct the signer to use the "Trustee" in their signature, and sometimes I don't.

And, for another curve ball, sometimes the lender will not require the trustee verbiage on any of their documents, but the title/escrow company will require it on their small bundle of documents. It is my pleasure to be of service and do as they ask...

TRUST DOCUMENTS YOU MIGHT SEE

In your closing documents, you may see a few additional pages for trust signings. The first will likely be with the Note and Deed of Trust/Mortgage document. Each of these usually has a Trust Rider that *rides along* with additional stipulations and clarity.

There will likely be a Trust Certification document that the borrower has already filled out once or twice before. Hopefully, the copy in your loan document package is the completed version. Sometimes, all lines are blank again and the borrower needs to do their best to fill it out again.

In many cases, possibly depending on the state you are in, the borrower may also need to fill out the Beneficiary Information form. This asks for names and addresses of the current beneficiaries. Please keep in mind that the borrowers in front of you may actually be the current beneficiaries of the trust. I know this can get confusing. This is by no means a legal advice book, but knowing this can actually help prompt the signer when they are equally confused. In the worst-case scenario, offer to call the closing agent and let the borrower explain why they do or do not understand this document.

Trust documents often may require a borrower to sign a document two or three times, in each of their capacities. They may sign as the individual, the trustee, and the settlor. If logic prevails, and the borrower signs in one line for both individual and for trustee, there will probably be another line for them to sign as settlor, at least on a few documents.

The trust settlor is simply the creator of the trust in this case.

BUSINESS ENTITY SIGNINGS

Sometimes companies, like an LLC or a Corporation, buy real estate, too. For the signing appointment, you'll meet the representative of the company that can sign legal contracts, often the owner, member, manager, or officer of the company.

For the most part, your documents are going to look just like the documents for a regular consumer mortgage because that is exactly what it is. The only difference is that the borrower is signing in the capacity of an officer or member of a company this time. For clarity sake, I am *not* talking about commercial loan transactions where the collateral is a piece of commercial property. I am talking about a single-family home or condo (or whatever) that just happens to be purchased by a business entity.

These signings are common and are similar to the trust signings we discussed previously, in that there is not a standard way to have them signed. Each lender is different. They may have Member, Manager, President, Principal, Partner (or more) typed after their name below the signature lines. How the lender wants them to sign will vary. Here are some possible ways your borrowers may have to sign documents for a business entity signing:

John Smith, Member

John Smith, Manager

John Smith, President

John Smith, Principal

John Smith, Partner

With these business entity signings, it is a good practice to just confirm with the closing agent exactly how they want the documents signed ahead of time. You can ask this question in a way that is professional and prudent to the situation: "Hi Jane, this is Bill, the mobile notary for the Smith signing happening tomorrow at 2pm. I just had a quick question; do you have a minute?" Of course, she does! "It seems like every lender is different these days. Would you like the borrower to use the suffix (member, Manager, Principal, etc.) in their signature?"

A good closing agent will appreciate you calling for clarity.

CASH TRANSACTIONS

For a "cash" transaction, there is very little paperwork because the buyer (not borrower) is outright paying cash for a property, so there is no lender. No lender means no government disclosures about...lending. Yay!

These cash signings range in pages from 5 or 6, to up to 20-30, depending on the closing agent and state.

Because there is very little paperwork, cash signings tend to go significantly faster. I've had buyers literally sit down, take a quick peek at the documents, just to be sure the numbers are right, and then sign everything in 10 minutes.

I've also had buyers that analyze every single line of their Settlement Statement. If something doesn't seem right to them, they will make calls to their real estate agent or closing agent, or even their attorney. That could stretch these signings to over an hour.

Don't sweat it.

If I was dropping a few hundred thousand bucks or even a million dollars in cash on a property, I might take a few extra minutes to make sure the paperwork was right, too.

SELLER SIGNINGS

If there is a buyer of a property, *someone* is a seller. On the seller side of a real estate transaction there is a *lot* less paperwork, too. This can vary from state to state, and from closing agent to closing agent, but count on 20-30 pages.

Sellers usually get a copy of the Settlement Statement, several disclosures, and then a form asking how they used the property for 2 of the past 5 years. This is an IRS tax reporting document, so the government knows how to tax the proceeds from the sale of the home. I won't get into that here, and nor should you in a signing. We just recommend they seek advice of a tax or legal professional.

WRAPPING UP YOUR SIGNING APPOINTMENT

When I started really taking my business seriously, I adopted a policy of *quadruple* checking my documents before they get dropped off for shipping or at the client's office. I call it my Q4 policy and it has saved my rear-end *many* times.

It doesn't matter how long you've been doing this, or how great you are at it, things slip by sometimes, especially if you are connecting well with the client.

Your first check of the documents should be done while the signer is signing, and immediately after the signing of each document. You want to check each document right then and there, as you move through the signing. Here's what your checking for:

(Keep in mind every document requirement is different so only use what applies)

- Signature is there.
- Signature matches ID and is the correct name (yes, people mess this up all the time).
- If necessary, middle initials are used.
- They date when needed.
- They didn't date where it isn't called for (especially important on the Note).
- The date is correct.
- Initials are in place when necessary.
- Any corrections are also initialed.
- You've signed and dated if necessary.
- You've notarized if necessary.
- Any blank lines that should be filled in are filled in.

In essence, you are really training your eyeballs to "hunt and destroy" blank lines. I like to look at every blank line on a document and consciously decide whether or not it requires action.

The second time you are going to review the documents is right there at the table with the borrower present.

I'll say something like, "Alright, we are all done! If it is okay with you, I am going to go through and check all of the documents again, just to be sure we didn't miss anything. Better to catch it now!" No one has ever disagreed with this.

Take your time and review every single page again. It takes less than 5 minutes.

We'll talk about the third and fourth time to check the documents coming up in the next two sections.

MACGYVER NOTARY TIP

Avoid using brightly colored sticky notes, or stickers that say, "Sign Here," or "initial here." Using stickers and sticky notes takes a tremendous amount of time to prep ahead of the loan signing appointment. And when you use tools like this, you are training your eyes and brain to look for bright sticky notes instead of blank lines. Case in point, when I first started mentoring and training notaries in Phoenix, the first "batch" really felt strongly about using sticky notes to remind them of where borrower's need to sign. Using these labels does bring a certain peace of mind...until you have to do a signing without them. Then, because their eyes were trained to look for the wrong things, their signings were riddled with errors.

PROCESSES AFTER THE SIGNING

Once I've closed the signing, shook hands, congratulated the signer (if it applies), and double-checked the documents for errors, I head out to my car.

If I am parked right in front of the signer's house (remember, we don't park in the driveway), I may actually pull around the corner or just a little further down the street. I like to do the next four steps out of view of the signer, so I am not parked in front of their house. Have you ever had someone leave your home and just sit out in front of your house for 15 minutes? It can be uncomfortable or weird for some people, so I just eliminate that possibility. Sometimes, I'll even run around the corner to a coffee shop for these next steps, too. The idea is to stay close to the borrower, just in case.

THE FOUR STEPS AFTER A SIGNING

For me and my clients, there are four things I need to do after every single signing. These might vary for you and your clients. Every client can be different.

The real take-away I hope you get here is the power of habits and routine. These four habits, strung together after each and every signing, have become a post-signing ritual. As far as my mind is concerned, I've automated and systemized my process.

As soon as I sit down behind the wheel and my car door shuts, I:

1. Securely upload or send the ID (if Applicable).
2. Create and Send an Invoice for the Signing or update my internal records. I'll share some thoughts and resources on this in Phase 5.
3. Check the Documents for errors. You've stayed nearby for a reason! This should be your third time checking those things.
4. Send a thank you card, or a, "nice to meet you," card to the signers. If this is for a new client/closing agent, I will send them one, too. This one practice has deepened my relationships and increased my revenues to untold amounts.

RETURNING THE DOCUMENTS

As the signing agent, it is your responsibility to return the documents to the closing agent or lender as directed. For clients that are out of your state, this usually entails dropping the document package at a shipping carrier like FedEx or UPS. They will typically include a shipping label and instructions for what to do. In most cases, you do not have to pay for shipping. Please note: there are some exceptions for this, but they are rare. In any case, be sure the documents are securely packaged, and there is a tracking number that proves you have dropped them off.

Your shipping materials are free from shipping carriers like FedEx and UPS (and others) so please do not skimp here. Get an envelope that actually fits the paperwork (never fold it). I've even known some signing agents to "double bag" their documents. They will put the docs in the firmer, tighter fit cardboard envelopes, then surround that package with a larger plastic, or the meshy fiber envelopes, just to be sure docs arrive safe and secure.

Just to reiterate: *always get a tracking number.* If it cannot be avoided, I will never leave docs in a night drop without evidence of doing so. That means I may take a picture of the actual night drop box with the "Last Pick Up" day and time obvious. I want my client to know I was there and fulfilled my duty.

For local clients, they may have a secure drop box location. They could also send a courier to you to pick them up. For me, I added document drop off to my menu of services and it has made all the difference, especially for new home purchases.

At first, I started doing this as a free value add. I worked with a client that was reluctant to do mobile signings because their transactions usually closed and funded the same day. When transactions close this soon after signing, there is very little margin for error, and it is critical documents get returned to the closing agent as soon as possible to begin the closing and funding process. I was able to build in the document delivery to my logistics. I ask my escrow client when the latest the documents could arrive on their desk and still get funded that day. Then, I knew the cushion of time I have had available for scheduling.

This created tremendous value for both the closing agent and the signer. The signer, or borrower, gets the luxury and convenience of a mobile notary service and the closing agent looks good to their client (the borrower). The closing agent also saved a ton of money on courier and delivery fees because I did not charge them. Eventually, recognizing the value they received, these closing agents increased my signing fees any time they could. *They* increased *my* fees. I was charging the standard $150 per signing, and these escrow officers had my back, increasing my signing fees to $200-$300 per signing. This is a perfect example of how to build a value-driven win-win relationship.

MACGYVER NOTARY TIP

You should check the documents one more time before you drop them at the closing agent or delivery service. This should be the fourth time you check the documents for errors.

FAX BACKS/SCAN BACKS

Some companies may require you to fax or scan/email certain documents from the loan package. If required, these documents usually consist of the most critical documents or the documents that are required for funding the loan. This way, the lender can be processing the loan for closing during the day or two the original documents you are sending over are in transit with the shipping/deliver company.

Sometimes, these fax/scan backs are 50 pages, and other times, they could be the entire loan package (200+ pages). For this reason, it can serve you to have a high-speed document scanner. It's also important to note that these fax/scan back requirements typically come from signing company relationships only. When you sign directly with escrow companies, there isn't usually a requirement for this. If there is a requirement from the lender, the closing agent or escrow officer, will handle it.

Once the documents are en route, your role is all about complete.

HANDLING ERRORS AFTER THE FACT

On occasion, you will make an error on a document. Some of these errors may be "critical," meaning the loan cannot close or fund until it is resolved. Other errors are less critical but still need to be resolved. Sometimes, a lender, closing agent or signing company may have you fix them. There will be times, a document may be able to be emailed directly to a signer for resolution, so they won't require you to do anything.

If you are contacted because of an error you made, regardless of your opinion on the matter, drop everything and fix it. Too many signing agents get caught up in a drama story or become argumentative. This is very short-sighted. *Always* keep the big picture in mind. When you are correcting an error on a document, you're not only mending the transaction, you are strengthening the relationship you have with the people who hired you. When you take ownership of your mistakes and go out of your way (at your expense in time and resources) to resolve them immediately, this resonates with your clients. They don't expect perfection. Errors will happen. How you get them resolved makes *all* the difference.

WHERE TO GET ADDITIONAL TRAINING

I'll make a few recommendations for online signing agent training. First, let me say that if your state offers specific notary training, whether free or otherwise, you should take that right away. These state-specific courses are often offered direct from the state or are sanctioned by the state. By taking this state-specific training, you'll know what is expected of you as a notary operating in your state. As I have mentioned before in this book, state requirements vary widely, so this is important. No training course can offer 50 different state-specific scenarios for you, so this responsibility is all yours.

As far as the loan signing agent training, this is a little different. The standards of practice, set mostly by the National Notary Association, and The Signing Professionals Workshop (SPW), are applicable in nearly every state, so it's much easier to teach and share how to do that practically anywhere in the United States. Still, some states regulate notary signing agents more than others, so, again, do your research.

SIGN & THRIVE NOTARY TRAINING COURSE AND COMMUNITY

This is the course I designed in early 2017. It is structured more like a learning community that you stay a part of for as long as you'd like. This book is modeled after the five phases that I teach in the course. In addition to the regulatory concerns, and the best practices that other courses teach (like the NNA), my course gets *very* detailed in exactly what to do during every single signing, before, during, and after.

But that's just one part of your role as a business owner. You still have to connect with industry leaders, build relationships, get more business, track your mileage, file and pay your taxes, build a team, bill your customers, open bank accounts, and so much more. My course combines online video modules, live webinars, live workshops, and our incredible private Facebook Group to help you learn and get the support you need. The environment is positive and collaborative, and we share information more than any online notary community I've ever seen. We also emphasize personal growth to fuel business growth, and we help facilitate that growth every day.

There is a small monthly subscription fee for Sign & Thrive which gives you access to everything. For more information, visit the resource page for this book.

CAROL RAY & NOTARY2PRO

Carol and I connected in early 2018 as two course creators committed to helping our students succeed. Carol is in this for all the right reasons and genuinely cares about her students.

The Notary2Pro loan signing training is nationally recognized and respected throughout the industry. Carol's training will take you from beginning to end, laying the foundation for a prosperous business. Because of her commitment to her students, you can count on incredible support that is just a phone call away (She still enjoys talking on the phone!).

I collaborate with Carol on many notary training projects that are available for free on YouTube. You can check those out, as well as her website on this book's resource page.

If your budget allows, you could take Carol's Notary2Pro and my Sign & Thrive Notary Course. That would give you a well-rounded perspective on starting and growing your new notary business. You would be light years ahead of others!

LAURA BIEWER AT COACHMELAURA.COM

I have the good fortune of collaborating with Laura Biewer on a variety of projects. She's a notary that is an expert in her field, especially when it comes to notary law. She's made a point of creating a sustainable business for herself that is balanced between general notary work and loan signings. On top of that, she offers individualized coaching and training courses to help with specific aspects of this business. You can take a Living Trust class, a POA and Medical Directive Class or a variety of others. Plus, as a certified instructor with the National Notary Association, her experience is invaluable in all 50 states. For a link to her website, please visit the resource page.

THE NATIONAL NOTARY ASSOCIATION

I mentioned before how valuable I think the National Notary Association is. They provide an astonishing amount of resources to notaries and signing agents, even if you are not a member. They establish the best practices for the industry, so their training is spot on. Their training is great for the general, technical and regulatory aspects.

If you have the budget to purchase three or four of these trainings, you will have a significant advantage in the industry. This is one of the reasons I priced the Sign & Thrive course at a small monthly fee ($33.00 per month as of this writing). I want you to be able to get the training you need *and* invest in marketing, infrastructure, and more training if you want it.

Training & education can be helpful. It can also be a trap. Watch out for analysis paralysis or "certification collecting." Sometimes we use pursuit of education as an excuse to avoid starting. Pick a trainer or mentor that resonates with you and has the service level you require and appreciate. Start there and add-on later.

MACGYVER NOTARY TIP

Phase 3 is huge and important. This is the work you will be doing all day, every day. Spend some time with this. As I mentioned earlier, there is no way I could include every possible document, for every possible lender and closing agent, for every single state, in this book. We are just scratching the surface here. I know it may feel like you're drinking from a firehose right now, but you'll want to make a note to come back to this section. To really step into your greatness, find a study-buddy. Find a friend, a relative, a kid, or a spouse, to practice this material with. Worst-case, use a mirror and practice to yourself! You don't need anyone to try and "trip" you up with trick questions or anything like that. All you need is someone who will sit there with their mouth shut and let you practice your script while you push paper back and forth. Believe it or not, where you choose to sit, how to start the signing, and navigating the paper-pushing, are three things that can jam you up the most...if you don't practice.

PHASE 4-
BUSINESS AND PROFESSIONAL
DEVELOPMENT

"What you get by achieving your goals is not as important as who you become by achieving your goals."

—Zig Ziglar

INTRODUCTION TO PHASE 4

Phases 1-3 have prepared you for *this*- getting new clients and maintaining an awesome relationship with them. In essence, the previous phases were helping you *become* who you needed to be in order to reach out to signing companies and closing agents with confidence.

This process of *becoming* will be ongoing as you advance yourself and your business to the next level. I whole-heartedly subscribe to the Japanese philosophy of Kaizen- constant, continuous, improvement. I encourage you to do the same. There is always a way to do things better and more efficiently!

In Phase 4, we are going to dive deep into what it takes to truly be exceptional in this business. We are going to show you how to move from transactional contractors to being the go-to, *requested* mobile notary for your clients.

Through authentic connection, a commitment to win/win interactions, consistent daily action, and creative innovations, I am going to show you how to build the foundation for your four pillars of relationship building. Here's what closing agents and signing companies are looking for:

COMPETENCY

You have to know how to do the task at hand, it's that simple. That's why training and experience is so important to industry influencers and leaders.

CONFIDENCE

You have to portray and demonstrate that competence to your signers, clients, and prospective clients in a gentle and non-threatening way. This is how you create smooth and efficient signings.

INTEGRITY

Integrity encompasses a lot. At its core, it just means, do what you said you'd do. And, if you can't, you must communicate and "re-negotiate." This may include:

- Showing up on time.

- Dressing in conformance to dress code.
- Knowing what you can do, and what you cannot do as a Notary Public.
- Dropping documents off on time.

Never, ever, ever, ever, sacrifice your integrity for anyone, including yourself.

LIKEABILITY

People work with who they *like, know, and trust.* Whether we agree with it or not, likeability is probably the biggest factor here. You could be strong in all three of the other pillars. Maybe you're great at what you do and how you do it. Perhaps you may be confident in those abilities and really know how to take gentle control of a signing. And, maybe you have impeccable integrity too. But, if you are a real jerk to work with, you'll be out of business in no time.

SELF-AWARENESS

Before we dive-in to relationship-building, marketing, and advertising, let's talk about you. What do you think about all day? Do you know how you show up to the world?

This is called self-awareness- your ability to observe what is happening inside your mind, check-in with alignment of principles and values, and adjust accordingly. In other words, how do you "control" that little voice in your head?

Are you able to pick up on other people's reaction to you, your words, your actions? Are you aware that people have stopped listening to you because you are rambling? Have you shared inappropriate information for that particular conversation? Are you avoiding eye contact?

Do you take responsibility for your emotional "wake?" Are you a tyrant, that leaves a trail of devastation depending on your moods? Or do you love too much, coming across as "needy" or "clingy?"

Self-awareness is a cornerstone to emotional intelligence, or EQ. Why am I talking about it in a book about how to build a mobile notary and loan signing business? Because all the marketing and advertising in the world won't matter if people don't want to do business with you because you're a jerk.

No one sets out to be a jerk, or to be clueless. It's often times just a lack of self-awareness and projection. Sometimes, we just assume that everyone else is like us and appreciates giving and receiving information the same way. That's not true.

While we never want to lose ourselves trying to be everything to everyone, there is tremendous power in knowing who we are and how we show up. Knowing our impact on the people around us can help us (and them) succeed. Understanding how we might use our strengths and weaknesses to better serve our clients, will help us stand out.

Volumes and volumes of books have been written on self-awareness and emotional intelligence already, so I won't write another one here. Instead, I'll point you in the direction, and give you a few of my favorites to read and implement on your own. I encourage you to build in reading/listening to these books every day as part of your skill development.

Reading List to get you started:

- "Emotional Intelligence: Why It Can Matter More Than IQ" by Daniel Goleman.
- The Harvard Business Review's "Emotional Intelligence Collection." (3 Books).
- A Cornell University study found that a high self-awareness score was *the* highest predictor of success in business owners and executives. This is a big deal.

Additional ways to learn more about yourself:

DISC

This section was contributed by friend and author, Sally Anders.

Being a Solopreneur is the dream of many. Succeeding in your own business requires two important fundamental skills. #1 – Know yourself – Is your natural style going to propel your success, or impede it? #2 – Know how to connect with others. That includes clients, as well as those who can help you succeed. RealSolutions, a Solopreneur, has the tools to accomplish both. The research-validated *Everything DiSC Workplace©* Profile* provides a personalized, 20-page report full of insights to better understand yourself, and others, as well as actions you can take to strengthen all of your relationships. Discover the strengths of your DiSC style, and how overusing those strengths can spell disaster. Learning the similarities and differences of the four DiSC styles is the short-cut to positive, productive, effective, and rewarding long-term relationships with your clients, and those wonderful people who support your dream. Your *ETDiSC Workplace* includes unlimited access to some *free* follow-up reports, and MyEverythingDisc website, an interactive *free ETDiSC* portal that helps you access DiSC strategies *long into the future* whenever a new *people* challenge arises! Thereby, making learning to communicate more effectively with *ETDiSC*, an investment that pays dividends for years to come.

You can learn more on the resources page for this book.

* A John Wiley & Sons, Inc. Publishers Product; RealSolutions, an Authorized Wiley Partner.

THE ENNEAGRAM

This section was contributed by friend, author, and coach, Linda Frazee.

The Enneagram is a powerful personality system of understanding not just what you do, but why you do it! Discover your blind spots, deepest motivation, and why you get triggered by certain people and situations. Step into yourself on a deeper level and learn how to get out of your own way! One of the best Enneagram coaches in the country is my life and business coach, Linda Frazee. Check out the resource page for more information!

THE VIA INSTITUTE

This incredible organization has a free test to help you categorize and rank your character strengths. I use this to help plan my annual learning and reading list. More info on our resource page.

ROCKSTAR ACADEMY AND THE "UNLEASH YOUR GREATNESS COURSE," BY DUSTIN HOGAN

Dustin Hogan is professional speaker, trainer and coach with a passion and obsession for personal growth and development. Through his inspirational seminars, coaching and online content Dustin empowers people to live inspired lives!

Over the years, on his own path of personal development, Dustin realized that there are specific strategies, insights, and philosophies that can be used on a daily basis to not only pursue your dreams, but to live your best life!

And this is why he created his course Unleash Your Greatness!

Unleash Your Greatness, is a 5-Week online course designed to assist you in creating a compelling vision for your life, cultivating powerful habits of success, and developing an action plan to pursue your goals and dreams!

Unleash Your Greatness takes a disciplined and practical approach to your growth and development. This allows you to create breakthroughs in all areas of your life that actually stick!

FINDING CLIENTS

Your strategy for finding clients will depend a lot on the goals of your business. Let's take a look at those three business models I mentioned at the beginning of the book and see which one works best for you.

INDEPENDENT CONTRACTOR FOR EXISTING SIGNING COMPANIES

Working as an independent contractor for existing companies can be an excellent way to "get your feet wet" after training as a loan signing agent. For my signing company, I welcome fresh new energy and a hungry-for-business attitude, and there are many more like me. Sure, there will be some companies that insist on experience first, and that's okay, too. You can grow into those.

These signing companies already have the relationships with Closing Agents in place, so they often have the consistent volume you'll be looking for as a new signing agent. Once you apply, or get "approved" with a signing company, they will notify you (and several others like you) of signing opportunities in your area, along with the compensation offered. The first one to respond, or whomever has the best rapport with the scheduler, will likely get the order.

The downside? Because of the efforts the signing companies put into acquiring and maintaining their relationships with their customers, they take a piece of the action for every signing. For example, if a signing company gets paid $150 for a signing, they may pay you $100 (or less) to facilitate it for them.

ESCROW OR CLOSING AGENT DIRECT

When you work directly with escrow officers, or closing agents, you are responsible for getting out and finding, meeting, connecting, servicing, and maintaining relationships with them and their team. There is a *lot* of joy and reward in this, especially if you're a people person.

It can also be lucrative, as in the example I used before, because there is no signing company middle-man now, *you* get paid the full $150 signing fee.

The downside? Relationships, while amazing in so many ways, are also fickle. Sometimes your favorite client gets laid off, fired, retire, gets mad at you (or her boss does), and sometimes your stomach starts to flip (not in a good way) when a certain client calls, and you decide to fire your client. It's business, and it's not for everyone.

Escrow Officers don't like to hear "no." They have their own clients to serve and need a loan signing agent that can deliver excellent service on *their* schedule. If you have a restricted schedule, like a full-time job or other commitment, this business model may not be for you.

THE HYBRID BUSINESS MODEL

In the hybrid business model, you get the best of both worlds. You can start out with signing companies, learn the ropes and, more importantly, discover which companies you most enjoy working with. Then, as your confidence builds, and your network expands, you can start networking and connecting with closing agents to go direct.

This is the business model I adopted...eventually. When I first started out, I had no idea there were signing companies even in existence. I thought we all had to go out and get our own clients all the time. As soon as I learned these companies were around, I lucked out with two that I absolutely *loved* to work with.

In my highest revenue producing year, I had only four clients- two escrow direct clients, and two signing companies. You see, you don't always need dozens of clients to hit or exceed your goals. Sometimes, you just need a few of the *right* ones.

WHO'S GOT MY MONEY?

I am a reader. I love reading books. One of the authors I've read lately is Grant Cardone. He gets lots of mixed reviews out there. Love him or despise him, he's a prolific marketer and writer.

One of the concepts I read about in the *Millionaire Booklet* was "Who's Got My Money?" This strategy helps clarify who your ideal customer is, so you can *highly* target your energy and resources when it comes to marketing, advertising, and relationship building.

It asks the question: "Who pays me for my service?"

That was extremely helpful to me, and I know it will be to you, too, regardless of the level of your business.

One of the cool things about being a loan signing agent is that our ideal customers, or "who's got our money," are crystal clear. We know that closing agents and signing companies are the people who hire us. Then, we can get creative and add some peripheral contacts there.

Once we have this clarity, we can create our marketing and networking strategies.

YOUR IDEAL CUSTOMERS

Okay, so we know "who's got our money." Closing Agents and signing companies are going to hire us. Within that criteria, you can get as specific as you'd like to when you choose the type of client you want to work with.

You could say you want to work with five of the Top 20 Closing Agents in Houston.

Or, I want a Closing Agent that enjoys Happy Hour with Me twice a month.

Or I work with closing agents and signing companies that are committed to win/win and long-term business relationships through growth and continuing education.

I encourage you to get as specific as you can. One of the traps of our business is that we get so hungry for new clients when we start up our business, we forget our own value and end up working for jerks or working for *far less* than our time and expertise is worth. Having some clarity about our ideal customer can bring us back.

SIGNING COMPANIES

There are hundreds of signing companies, or signing *services* as they are often referred to, across the country. There are several cool things about working with these existing companies:

First, it doesn't matter where the signing company is *physically* located. Even though their home office may be located in Modesto, they could potentially have signers in every nook and cranny of the country.

Second, signing companies have done all the relationship building for you. All you have to do is show up and do the work with pride.

Third, some of these signing companies have massive volume because of the efforts they make on the relationship side. This can keep you busy.

Fourth, signing companies can be a *lot* more forgiving when it comes to errors and mistakes. We all know that mistakes can happen. Because of the volume of signings that signing companies see, you'll likely be okay for future signings- as long as your attitude about fixing them is positive and timely.

Fifth, if you can only start out part-time, working for signing companies is just about your only option. They don't take it personally (usually) if you're not available. They just move on to the next signing agent in line.

And finally, working with signing companies is like having a paid internship. The fees may be lower than if you got the business directly from a closing agent, but you are gaining valuable knowledge, insight, experience, and *confidence*. All of this will be necessary as you expand your business to the escrow/closing direct business model.

HOW TO CONNECT

Depending on the business model you choose, you'll want to sign up with anywhere from 2-100 of these signing companies. Yup, I said 100.

If your goal is to get your phone Ringin' & Dingin' to generate revenue, then increase the chances of that happening by signing up with more companies. This becomes even more important for those who are working part time. You have to increase the odds of a signing coming in at a time you are available. It's a numbers game at that point!

Most signing companies have some sort of application process that will require you to submit evidence that you are a Notary Public, and you have the correct insurances and bonds, if necessary. Here's what you can expect to submit (some companies require more, some less):

- A copy of your Notary Public Commission.
- Evidence of Errors & Omissions Insurance.
- Evidence of Criminal Background Check Clearance.
- If E-Notary, may have to provide that license or certificate as well.

In addition to providing these documents, you'll also be asked a series of questions about your fees for certain services, which counties or zip codes you're willing to work, and more. In a lot of ways, and for a lot of these signing companies, this is very similar to applying for a job. The information is the same, and there is a lot of repetition as you progress through the various companies.

This can feel super tedious, and many people quit applying after 10-15 companies. These are the same people that complain that there isn't enough business out there.

Keep going! You absolutely get to decide how many signing companies you want to sign up with, and how you want to grow your business. There are ways that work faster than others. If you want signing opportunities, sign up with at least 100 of these signing companies.

The good news is, once you sign up and get approved, you are in! All you have to do is update your credentials with renewal information each year.

WHERE TO FIND SIGNING COMPANIES

I mentioned earlier that there are hundreds, maybe even thousands, of signing companies throughout the country. Some are large companies with cool software and smartphone apps to distribute their signing offers. Some, are small, Mom & Pop type companies that barely have a web presence (so they're hard to find).

You are in this business for yourself, but you are not in it *by* yourself. There is a community of loving and supportive notaries that are sharing information to help you succeed and thrive.

One such group, led by Carrie Rivera out of Illinois, is *Notary Reviews- The Good, The Bad, and The Ugly* (on Facebook). In this private group, designed only for active loan signing agents, members can share their experiences with signing companies all over the United States in a safe environment, free from retaliation by the signing companies they may review.

In her premium service, available on her website, Carrie has a whole community with additional resources, including her list of star-rated signing companies and how to contact them. This is an invaluable resource for a loan signing agent, regardless of experience level. Check out the resource page for a link to Notary Reviews.

SIGNING COMPANY FEES TO EXPECT

When it comes to the fees you can expect from signing companies, there is a full range. Depending on the type of signing and the company you are working for, the fees could range anywhere from $50-$125.

One of the benefits of working with signing companies is that you can decline loan signing offers that do not make financial sense to you. If a signing offer comes in at $75, but requires a two-hour drive, one way, you can decline the offer. Maybe you're not the ideal "signer" for that offer.

The important thing to do is to *always* respond to offers, even if you can't take them. Be polite. Make a counter-offer if reasonable. But, do not ignore offers. When you ignore, the systems *can* start to recognize that and assume you are no longer interested in business.

GETTING PAID BY SIGNING COMPANIES

Each signing company has their own payment policies. Some will pay you upon the closing of the loan you signed. Some will pay bi-weekly, and some every 30-45 days or longer. It just depends. When you sign up, and get accepted with a signing company, they will usually clarify their payment policy.

THE DIRECTORIES

Within the industry, there are several directories that a notary can register with and create a business profile that will help potential customers. Many of these are free, at least at a basic level. Many have an enhanced profile option they offer at an additional fee.

Both consumers *and* Closing agents have been known to use well-known and established directories to find the notary and signing agent they need in any given area. With a reputable directory, you can get a consistent flow of customers.

There are a *lot* of directories out there. I don't want to take away anything from the start-ups that may have a lot to offer- I just don't know who they are yet. So, I am going to share the top three directories that have a free profile option *and* their paid upgrades typically pay off for us.

1. NotaryCafe

2. Notary Rotary

3. 123Notary

SCAM WARNING

While there are many directories that aim to provide legitimate services, there are some directories that are borderline frauds. They charge you an annual or monthly fee and promise that 100% of signing fees are paid to you. Then you never hear anything from them except to charge your card again. They have a non-existent base of customers, so your phone never rings, either. These companies choose a fee that you can easily justify paying, especially if you are brand new. Beware.

The best resources are your peers and colleagues. This is where having a community of like-minded, supportive notaries can give you the information you need to avoid (hopefully) these companies that aim to take advantage of us.

MAJOR PLATFORMS

The rise of technology platforms, such as Snapdocs, is changing the industry significantly. Snapdocs is a central "hub" that signing companies and closing agents (like escrow officers and attorneys) can use to disseminate their loan signings. In fact, other companies can distribute opportunities to us here, too, like debt resolution appointments, field property inspections, and more. I'll go into a little more detail on those appointments in the Side-Hustle Lounge section of this book.

Notaries can sign up with Snapdocs (and others like it) relatively easily by creating a profile and uploading required credentials.

As loan signing (or other) appointments become available in your area, the closing agent or signing company "pushes" the appointment out to you and others in the proper zip code. The "first" signing agent to either respond, or the first to connect with the scheduler on that appointment, gets the appointment.

This little section of the book is not designed to be a full description of how this business model works or how the technology itself works, but it is important you know it exists. It is also important that you have a grasp of some of the pros and cons of a technology platform, like SnapDocs.

PROS

There are some pretty obvious pros to technology platforms like this. One, you can register just once and have access to hundreds (maybe thousands) of signing closing agents and signing companies. This can be very convenient.

Second, this technology makes communication between the parties, including sending and receiving documents easier to both read, deliver, and archive.

Plus, they have record keeping and reporting built-in, so this can be helpful for tracking production and filing taxes.

CONS

These technology platforms, like SnapDocs, charge a fee to the companies that use their service. That is to be expected, of course. However, this becomes a "con" for notaries because that expense is actually passed on to us in the form of lower signing fees.

In the online forums, you'll see *lots* of conversation about "low-baller" fees from Snapdocs and similar tech platforms. It is important to distinguish SnapDocs, the technology platform, from the signing company or closing agent making the "low-ball" offer. You may find that many signing fees offered through the SnapDocs platform are less than stellar. But, not always! There are some very reputable companies that use these platforms and still pay fair fees for a mobile notary and loan signing agent.

My suggestion to you is to definitely register with these technology platforms, especially in the beginning of your career. Just know that companies like SnapDocs are *not* the end all, be all. Don't stop there. Too many new loan signing agents go through the whole process of becoming an NSA only to sign up for SnapDocs alone. Then...sit and wait for the phone to start ringing. It takes more.

Some of the most successful notaries using these technology platforms still use old-fashioned relationship skills to gain more business. They pick up the phone and call the scheduler to have a conversation about the signing or their availability. Or, whether they get the signing or not, they will send a greeting card, thanking for time or thanking for the signing. There is *always* a human being behind the technology, so this is *always* a relationship business.

POACHING

Poaching is the act of pursuing someone else's client as your own. Here's how that looks in our world.

You accept a signing offer from Signing Company A. You perform the signing, which happens to be for Best Bank Mortgage Company, with Dream Escrow Company as the closing agent.

In our industry, Dream Escrow Company is Signing Company A's client. One way or another, they have built a relationship with that company, and now get to facilitate signings by sub-contracting the work to people like you and me.

Poaching would happen if you call up the Escrow Officer for Dream Escrow Company and start talking about how great you are as a signing agent. Maybe you suggest they would cut Signing Company A out of the middle, and could just call you direct next time.

Tacky, tacky, tacky.

And, maybe even against the law, or against contracts, at the very least.

Don't do this. It makes you look *really* bad. A good escrow officer who values relationships is never going to do business with someone who so quickly bites the hand that feeds them.

Just show up as your best self, being of service. If a relationship naturally evolves, so be it. But do not actively pursue a signing company's client. And never sacrifice your integrity to get a client

---

MACGYVER NOTARY TIP

Sometimes just the perception of poaching can be enough to lose a client. Perception is reality. This shows up when you send a thank you card to that escrow officer for Dream Escrow Company, *instead* of sending it to the signing company that is technically your client. If Signing Company A even suspects you are trying to make a move on their clients, you can bet you are out of there.

There is plenty of business for everyone. Focus on building your own relationships.

CLOSING AGENTS OR ESCROW DIRECT

WHAT IS A CLOSING AGENT?

A closing agent is an impartial third party who facilitates the transfer of real estate. They are typically responsible for finalizing and providing paperwork to us. Then, they'll make sure that everyone who should be paid in a transaction does, in fact, get paid. In most cases, the closing agent will also be responsible for "recording" the documents with proper governments to finalize the transfer of property. This is usually done at the county level, but every state is different.

A closing agent will likely be one of two roles; either an escrow officer, or in some eastern states, an attorney, or "closing attorney."

ESCROW OFFICERS

Always remaining a neutral, impartial party, the Escrow Officer is usually an employee of an escrow/title company. Their responsibilities are to ensure that real estate contract stipulations, lender requirements, and state and local requirements, are satisfied before closing a real estate transaction.

Part of this responsibility is making sure that all documents are fully executed correctly. That's where signing agents, like you and me, come in.

In essence, you are representing the escrow officer at the closing table. That's why so many escrow officers can hesitate to use a "stranger" as a signing agent. They want someone they *know* will represent them well and make them look good.

Being an escrow officer is one of the most stressful jobs in the country. On top of the enormous responsibility of facilitating the transfer of enormous wealth and property in meticulous detail, they encounter personality types all across the spectrum. Some people are amazing. Some people are jerks. Closing real estate deals can bring out the best in people...and the worst. And escrow officers seem to take the brunt of a deal gone wrong.

Everybody throws escrow under the bus. Lenders blame escrow. Builders blame escrow. Real Estate agents...blame escrow. Consumers, who do not understand the process...blame escrow.

These escrow officers are put through the ringer, and, most of them *still* love what they do. They have thick skin and can take it. Still, the good ones that take ownership of their files, are almost OCD in their attention to detail, and take pride in a closing gone well.

These are the escrow officers I enjoy working with. Their time is valuable, so they appreciate me. They know I will represent them professionally and make them look *real* good.

CLOSING ATTORNEYS

In some states, known as "Attorney States," the law requires that an attorney be present or involved in the closing of a real estate transaction. In those states, the attorney essentially performs the duties of the escrow officer (or reviews them).

A real estate closing attorney will usually, examine the title, provide an opinion of the title for the insurance company, coordinate the parties involved, review the loan documents, records and distribute funds.

In most states, the Closing Attorney still uses loan signing agents, like you and me, to facilitate signings, and gather signatures. There are thriving signing agents in all 50 states. Still, the interpretation of the law that says that an attorney "must be present or involved" leaves a lot of gray area. Check with your local state government, state bar association, and a notary association to help you navigate. It will be difficult to get a straight answer, and I recommend you get a few opinions.

HOW TO FIND CLOSING AGENTS

Escrow officers and attorney's closing agents can be found all around us. Real Estate is a *huge* industry, and almost every one of those transactions requires a closing agent. We'll dive deeper into a few of these, as well as how to connect with them when you find them, in just a bit. For now, here are a few places you can find closing agents:

- Google Title/Escrow Companies or Real Estate Closing Attorneys
- LinkedIn
- Pretty much any business networking group

- Title/Escrow Associations
- Personal referrals

YOUR CONNECTION STRATEGY

Once you've decided that you want escrow direct business, meaning you intend to build relationships directly with closing agents, it's time to make a plan.

More so than any other business I've been involved in, my mobile notary and loan signing business is heavily reliant on strong, authentic relationships. Building relationships takes finesse, cultivation, authenticity, and patience. Because of this, I think many people do it "wrong." They overthink it, or they cut corners. Relationships, of all kinds (not just business) take time, and they are worth it!

As you build your strategy to connect, there are four "pre-requisites" I am going to ask that you adopt. These are foundational truths that will make all the difference as you work to build authentic relationships with closing agents.

THE FOUR PRE-REQUISITES

PRE-REQUISITE NUMBER ONE: TRACK YOUR NETWORK

You've probably heard that "your net worth equals your network." This rings true in our business, too. In fact, there's a really good chance that you already know people who know the people that could blow this business up for you.

Even if you don't know them just yet, there is a good chance you will meet them very soon. It's just how this business works...*when* you are open to opportunities.

Most of us have no idea how large our network really is. We have the same friends we hang out with, a few people we work with, and then our family, so we think we have an insignificant network. Think bigger here.

Create a "Contact List" of every single person you know-every single one. You don't have to organize it or label people, or even decide right now if you ever want to talk to them again. Right now, just make your list.

If it is easier, start in your closest circle and work out. Remember, we do not have to qualify anyone to be on this list. If you know them, they go on it. You can filter later.

Here are some prompts to help you:

- Who lives in my house?
- Who do I go to school with? Or...who *did* I go to school with?
- Who do I work with?
- Who is in my family? Who was at the family reunion last year?
- Who do I go to concerts with?
- Who gets invited to my parties?
- If I was going to get married next month, who would I invite?
- If I died tomorrow, who would be invited to the funeral?
- Who have I called on for sales?
- Who did I meet at the last networking event?
- Who is in my doctor's office?

It's easy for us to slip into the trap of qualifying people before we put them on the list. We discount people and our connection to them by saying, "Sure I know Bob, but Bob is a roofer and doesn't know anyone. What does he have to do with notary work?" Or, something along those lines. Step out of that role as a qualifier for this exercise.

When done correctly, you'll have a list of hundreds, perhaps thousands of names. In fact, various studies have shown that the average American knows between 290 - 600 people. You may fall on the low end here, and there are many of you that will exceed those numbers.

The value of your network is more than "who can pay me for my services." In a way, that is important, of course. We are in business, after all. Still, I encourage you to ask instead, "To whom can I be of service?" This shift in your thinking will change everything for you and make adding people to your list a lot more fun and rewarding.

When I first started this exercise, I used a legal pad to track all the names of people. I love the act of writing, so it really helps me process and remember. Still, a legal pad is not sustainable for long-term tracking. I learned that the hard way. I am one of those people with a significantly higher than average network. I love to meet new and interesting people, so my list is large.

After the legal pad, I switched to Excel for my contact list. And, eventually, I started using a CRM (Customer Relationship Manager) software. These days, you can get software like that for free, like HUBSpot, and it integrates well with Gmail.

Your CRM will help you organize and label your contacts. This is very helpful, but most importantly, a good CRM will help you automate your communication. Your ability to stay in touch, and Top of Mind, with your current and potential clients has a direct impact in achieving extraordinary results in this business.

Just about everything you read in Phase 4 of this Sign & Thrive system is designed to inspire creative and authentic ways to keep you Top of Mind with your contact list. That way, when there is an opportunity for a deeper relationship, you are positioned to take action and be of service.

PRE-REQUISITE NUMBER TWO: DON'T DO IT FOR THE MONEY

Since we keep talking about the importance of being of service, let's dive a little deeper into that now. As a mobile notary and loan signing agent, there is an opportunity to make a *lot* of money. For many of us, that is thrilling.

Heck, I even sub-titled the book, *How to Make Six Figures as a Mobile Notary and Loan Signing Agent.*

Still, while income can be substantial, and it is very important to long term sustainability, don't jump in here and just do it for the money. It won't work.

In a business so heavily reliant on authentic relationships, if you are here for the sole purpose of padding your checking account, people will pick up on that. They'll smell it on you. This is especially important when you're just starting out or otherwise rather desperate for cash flow. Your energy shifts when you come from a "lack" mentality.

Instead, come from an abundant mindset. Be here because of the service and impact you can make for the public you serve.

One of our greatest gifts as a mobile notary and loan signing agent is to help people when they need us most. Sometimes, that is the best day of their life, and sometimes, it's the worst. Honor that and the money will follow.

PRE-REQUISITE NUMBER THREE: HAVE A GREATER VISION FOR YOUR LIFE

We are all here, building this business for a reason, whether a divine one or a reason of our own choosing. Tap into that and remind yourself of what you want and who you want to be in this world. Then, write it down and refer to it every single day.

This is probably the most powerful of all these exercises, and it is also probably the most skipped step as well. Creating a vision statement for your life seems cheesy and "fluffy" to some people. Maybe they're right. However, I do not mind being cheesy and fluffy, living the life of my dreams, and you probably shouldn't mind that, either.

Successful people envision their life. They know what they want and why, even if they do not fully understand the "how" they'll get there just yet. That is okay. The "How" shows up when it needs to. Our job is to clarify what we want, who we are willing to become to make it happen, and why we want to do it.

Having a compelling "Why" will help get you out of bed in the morning. It will help you keep going, driving those long days. It will get you through those hard lessons. Your "why" will help you take just one…more…signing, especially when, you don't feel like it.

PRE-REQUISITE NUMBER FOUR: CONSISTENT ACTION

As you move deeper into Phase 4, we will have to come to an agreement. The agreement is that random, sporadic, actions, are *not* going to elevate you to success. You have to consistently move toward your dream, even if only inch by inch, every single day.

I used to ride the "inspiration wave" like a mad man. Maybe you've experienced those times in your life when you have the great ideas that keep you up all night, wheels turning, and your cranking out notes, and visualizing how something might work.

There is almost a "high" to this. The work is enjoyable. The possibilities are endless. Then…

The energy wains.

Sometimes the inspiration wave lasts an hour, sometimes it lasts a couple of weeks. When you're on it, it's easy to take consistent action because you are fired up.

The key to success in this, and any business, is maintaining that consistency, even when you no longer feel like doing it.

That's where having a little bit of structure, or a routine, in your day can change everything.

THE DAILY ROUTINE THAT CHANGED EVERYTHING

Earlier, I shared a little about my story starting out as a mobile notary and loan signing agent. My energy was distracted, and I didn't really respect this business for what it is. I treated it like an ATM machine, sporadically jumping in and out, mainly when I needed to make some fast money for the other 5 or 6 businesses I was trying to run.

As I mentioned in the previous section, random, sporadic, activity is not sustainable. Those other businesses began to crumble. Even my notary business began to falter because of my fragmented energy. In a relationship business, when you're working with people, they can pick up on your lack of presence and commitment, even if they can't tangibly explain it to you. They get a feeling, and it often times repels them from you.

So, I lost customers.

The other businesses I ran completely failed. There were five or six of them, and none of them were synchronistic with each other, so working on one, required all of my attention. I was pulled in too many directions.

I had one notary client that stuck with me, pretty much from the beginning though, averaging about $1,000 a month in revenue. That kept me alive…barely.

I was making about $1,000 a month as a notary, and my rent was $1,000 a month, so yeah, times were tight.

When your businesses fail, and you let the people you love down, hell, you let yourself down, your confidence crumbles. When your confidence crumbles, the dynamic you have in relationships changes. I felt like I was losing everything.

And, in many ways, I was.

It wasn't just these five or six business concepts. There had been twenty more before them!

And now, my personal relationships were suffering. People who had supported me through so much before were now starting to lose faith in my abilities. Who could blame them? 26 business failures? I think it was a gift to have so many who supported me for so long.

When your confidence is down, you put up with more than you should, sometimes, too. This led to a break-up in my personal life, too.

And there I was, alone, on a Thanksgiving weekend. I lied to those who loved me and told them I had lots of plans. And, technically, I did have plans, but delicious food, family, and football was not among them.

I was depressed and wanted to be alone.

If there is such thing as rock bottom, I think this was it for me.

My plan was to sulk for four days, when most people leave each other to themselves. Instead, I got a burst of inspiration to explore *why* this was happening, and why it had happened so many times before.

Why didn't I have everything I wanted?

I thought I was smart enough. I was well supported, in that people believed I could do these things. I wasn't afraid to try-hell, I had started 26 businesses!

Why couldn't I get the results I dreamed of?

So, the first thing I did was take a results inventory. I took a look at accomplishments, things I wanted, things I had, skills I had acquired, and skills I needed, and I wrote them all down on giant pieces of paper taped to the walls of my apartment.

Now, I had a much clearer picture of what I had, versus what I wanted. And the discrepancy was enormous.

Here I was, approaching forty years old, with this dream of being a successful serial entrepreneur, and I didn't have a "real" successful business. I was terrified that I was going to die with the song still inside me.

I started reading more books, watching TedTalks, exploring YouTube- whatever I could lay my eyes on about results and the lack thereof.

I learned that what I had resisted the entire first half of my life, healthy habits and routines, were directly correlated with affirmative results. Even writing that sentence now seems ridiculous. Seems kind of obvious, right? Maybe you're already one of the lucky ones who realized the power of positive habits and a success routine early in life, and this isn't news to you.

For me, it was groundbreaking. I mean, I think I "knew" that what I *should* have been doing every day. But, how that translated in real life, was completely different. I only worked on the "fun" stuff. Even then, I only worked when I was "inspired" to do so. Still, I allowed, maybe even invited, distractions into my life to avert the work. Talk about a self-sabotage cycle.

Maybe you can relate.

As I continued to read books like, *The Power of Habit* by Charles Duhigg, and *The Charged Life* by Brendon Burchard, and researching sites like BJ Fogg's *Tiny Habits*, something began to click for me. I had resisted habits and routines my whole life because I thought only boring people had routines. I thought the people with routines had given up their dreams and were missing out. It turns out, those with clarity enough of their dreams to create a string of habits (a routine) to reach those dreams actually, in fact, reach those dreams.

I dove deeper.

That's when I happened across another book about habits, routine, and the power of mornings, and this one, changed everything.

I don't have to re-hash the whole book here for you, as you can read or listen to it for yourself. The take-away today is that there is power in the mornings, and even if you are not a "morning person," you can change your life by implementing six powerful practices, before 8:00am.

I was one of those people who didn't much care for early mornings. One of those companies I told you I owned was a pub poker league that kept me out until one or two in the morning. The last thing I wanted to do was wake up at 5:00am.

But this strategy by Hal Elrod resonated with me. I knew that the only way anything was going to change is if I started changing the way I did things. So, I committed to the 30-Day Miracle Morning Challenge, and my entire life changed for the better.

These daily habits that Elrod calls the "S.A.V.E.R.S.", an acronym for Silence (Meditation, Prayer), Affirmations, Visualization, Exercise, Reading, and Scribe (Journal), are powerful enough on their own. Strung together as a morning routine, the impact is exponentially bigger.

These are the habits that help us *become* who we need to be in order to run successful businesses. These are the habits that improve self-confidence, increase self-awareness, and deepen relationships, both with ourselves, and with others.

Don't skip this step.

The difference between ordinary and extraordinary is this work right here.

Once I finished the 30-Day challenge, my businesses were still in turmoil, all but evaporated, but my confidence was solid. I didn't know exactly what I was going to do, but these SAVERS kept me anchored in the storm. I wasn't going backward ever again.

After the third or fourth month with Miracle Morning, I felt good, but still had no idea how I was going to make more money. The businesses were gone, not that they had provided any income in the first place, but I was struggling. I had one notary client who had stuck with me. Plus a few straggling referrals that made me a consistent thousand bucks a month or so. But when my rent was $1,000 a month too, I was still drowning.

That's when that fateful Sunday Funday conversation with Jamie changed everything. In between sips of beer, she said, "Why don't you focus all of your energy on this 'notary gig?' It's been the one business that seems to be working, no matter what."

I really did feel something click for me. What if I did take all of this business experience, all of this "book" knowledge I had, and applied it to this mobile notary and loan signing business? What could happen?

I spent the next few days with giant paper taped to my walls, devising a plan.

What I had learned from my results inventory, and lonely Thanksgiving weekend was that knowledge was useless without implementation. So, how could I make this round generate different results.

The SAVERS had me feeling good about me and the world, so I needed my own version of SAVERS for my business. These would be the daily habits that moved my business Foreword , no matter what, every single day.

I called them, my Daily Do's.

THE DAILY DO'S

There is a really good chance that you already know what it is you *should* be doing in your business every day, but you're not. I know I did at least have some sort of vague understanding that if I wanted to grow my business, more people needed to know about my business.

I started there and set a big goal for myself. I was broke, about to be destitute, so I knew I needed money fast and consistently. To me, a fledgling entrepreneur most of my life, the idea of making $100,000 a year seemed like the perfect, and somewhat out of reach, goal for me. It was a stretch, to say the least.

Then, I did the math on it.

$100,000 divided by 12 months equaled $8,333.33 per month, about $1900 per week. I was already making about $250 a week as a mobile notary and loan signing agent, so to hit my goal, I only needed to make an additional $1,650 every week.

Piece of cake...right?

I had never made anywhere near $2,000 a week, and here I was trying to ten X my income when I was at rock bottom.

At the time, I was working escrow direct, and was getting paid about $150 per signing, but a few were coming in at $75 (a very lowball contract I agreed to with a client). So, I used an average of $100 per signing.

At a hundred bucks a pop, I would need about 16 more signings per week, or about 3 more per day, Monday through Friday, in order to hit my $100,000 a year annual goal. Either that, or…I need to find a way to increase my fees.

So, the way I saw it, I had two clear paths to my goal: one, I needed to generate more signings every week, which meant more clients. And two, I needed to find a way to bring more value to my clients, so they would not hesitate to pay more for my services.

With that in mind, I worked my way backwards, or reverse-engineered those three goals, until I came up with, what I thought, should be daily action items to get me there. That is how the Daily Do's were born.

The results were stunning, to say the least. Within 90 days of implementing them, my relationships, both personal and in business, were deepened and solidified. My self-confidence and happiness were off the charts. And, my income soared from $1,000 a month to $20,000 a month in loan signing revenue.

There's been a little fluctuation through the years, but for the most part, income has stayed steady or increased, even after my main goals and objectives have shifted a bit.

MOVING THE NEEDLE

The following list of activities were on my radar every single day. These were the things I needed to do every day to move the needle on my $100,000 per year goal. I trusted that if I did each of these things, every day, the sun would not set without making massive movement toward the goal. That not only got the job done, but also let me sleep so much better at night. And, I did nearly all of this before 8:00am.

Your early mornings are important as a mobile notary and loan signing agent because as soon as escrow officers and signing company staff get into the office, your phone could be ringing and dinging all day. Own your day, and make sure everything that needs to move you Foreword toward your dream gets done, even if you get busy.

The following are my Daily Do's that you can use to help grow your business. These are scalable. You can do more than I did here, or you can do less. Adapt them to your goals.

ADD 3-5 NAMES

Remember the pre-requisites I talked about, where I recommended you track your network and keep a contact list? That's of critical importance if you want to achieve extraordinary results in this business. I kept mine on a legal pad (not recommended), and subsequently a Excel spreadsheet. I committed to adding at least 3-5 new names to this list every single day. This forced me to engage with people and lay the foundation of a great relationship. As an introvert, this was especially hard for me, but I worked on it, mainly by asking more questions of the other person, than by sharing more about myself. Remember, this list isn't *just* for business contacts. Include your personal contacts, too! As your business starts to gain traction, the list gets longer and longer. When you're out hustling and bustling as a mobile notary & loan signing agent, all we do is meet new people all day.

PING 10

Now that you have your contact list, and you're adding to 3-5 names a day, it is important to stay in touch with them. To help do that, practice the art of the "ping," or what I call, tickling. When you ping or tickle someone, you are just sending a quick reminder that you are thinking about them and care about them.

In many ways, you do this already for your closest inner circle, like your partner, your kids, your family, and friends. These little messages similar to, "Hey, how are you?" or "I was just thinking about you the other day. What's new?" are pretty natural in personal relationships. Expanding your circle to include people you don't know as well yet, and even your business contacts, will change your business forever.

Aside from just staying in touch with people, we ping to avoid being "that guy." You know the one- he only ever reached out to you when he has a new job, a new opportunity, or a new product to offer you. Don't be "that guy."

HOW TO PING

When you don't know the people you're pinging or tickling, the key is to be authentic and *not sell!* Selling is *not* what pinging and tickling is all about. We just want to stay in touch and cultivate a friendly relationship. To do this, find ways of being of value. Then start sharing it with the people on your contact list. Here are some ideas for Pinging, or tickling:

- Share and tag them in an article relevant to them.
- Ask them how they are doing.
- Follow up on a previous conversation.
- Ask them how you can support them in their business.
- Ask them what a good referral for them is.
- Connect them to people they can help or can help them.
- Ask them out to coffee, tea, or cocktails (whatever).
- Offer a reading list or ask them for one (if they are readers).
- Refer some business to them and help grow their business.

SEND 1-10 GREETING CARDS

This one practice alone changed everything for me. I decided to send out at least one thankyou card every single day, and then I ten X'd it for this little experiment. I was sending 1-10 of these greeting cards to possible business associates, current associates, and even friends and family, every day.

I know the results you probably want to hear are about the amount of business I generated doing this (which was, and continues to be, a *lot*), but the real value for me came with the enormous sense of gratitude and love I felt after *sending* the cards. You have to try it!

On top of the joy I feel sending them, the response is incredible. I've had clients call me in tears after receiving one of my cards. And, some still have cards up on their fridge at home, even if they don't work in the business anymore.

Greeting cards, and the authentic, deeper than "normal" message I can include in them, deepened *all* of my relationships and put me into gratitude first thing in the morning.

Since then, I now include a thank you card to either the signer or the escrow officer, in nearly every signing, when appropriate. Sometimes, if the situation calls for it, I send one to both the signer *and* the escrow officer. This is one of the first four things I do after a signing, while I am still in my car. That way I never forget!

Because I do this in my car, efficiency is very important. I choose to use a company with an amazing smartphone app that allows me to customize cards with fonts, words, and images. The company then sends a real card via the USPS to the recipient.

Again, it is important to be authentic and *not sell* anything in your cards. These are tools of connection, not sales. My cards are short and sweet, saying something like this:

"Congratulations on your new home! It was such a pleasure meeting you for your loan document signing the other day. I hope your move goes smooth and I can't wait to see how your landscaping looks next year!

Thank you!

Bill (The Notary)"

Or to escrow officers:

"Hi Jodi,

The Smiths were a delight to work with!

Thank you so much for the signing (and the organized file)!

Enjoy your end of month!

Bill (The Notary)"

OPTIONS FOR SENDING CARDS

There are all kinds of ways to send cards these days. Choose the one that fits your style and your budget. Remember, authenticity is key here, so it needs to fit your personality. I would also encourage you to use a system that is easy for you. If it's too clunky, you simply won't do it. That's human nature. Choose something easy for you to use.

HANDWRITTEN CARDS

This is probably the cheapest route, and there is a lot of value in handwriting your cards these days. This is also the chunkiest of the systems, at least for me. It's too messy to carry the cards, envelopes, and stamps, plus having a surface to handwrite cards on the fly, often while in the car. Still, very powerful if you can make it work.

TOUCHNOTE

This is a smartphone app that allows you to create custom postcards and greeting cards. Very popular! You create it on the app, and the pieces are mailed from a central location to your recipients.

SEND OUT CARDS

This is the system I used. I am impressed with the smart phone app, and the handwriting font selection, so it looks like the card is handwritten, even though it is not. With this technology, I can also instantly upload a picture of my client, us as a selfie (if we took one), and even their pets, which they *love*.

You can also become a referral partner for them and generate income every time someone buys the service using your link or website. My friend, Sara Basloe, is an expert on relationship marketing and Send Out Cards. Check out her link on the resources page.

STACKED MEETINGS & NETWORKING

Did I just say "networking?" My stomach used to turn at the thought of awkward rooms and name tags. If I am completely honest about it, my stomach *still* flips a bit for networking events. I am an introvert at heart and being in a room full of people I don't know, or that don't know me, completely wipes my energy.

Luckily, I've learned a lot about turning the traditional or stereotypical networking concept into something far more valuable, and even fun sometimes.

I am the type of person who will look for *any* excuse to get out of or avoid social situations. I knew I needed a strategy for networking that made it easy, relaxed, and fun for me. This was clearly not going to be a networking meeting…at first. I had to ease into it.

I found an interesting strategy in Michael Maher's book, "The 7 Levels of Communication." In fact, Maher's book inspired a few of my Daily Do's. If you want to dive deeper into building relationships, that would be the book to start with.

Maher described a "stacked meetings" day, where you schedule one-on-one meetings with a series of people you want to either connect with, or stay in touch with, at one particular location. You can be strategic with the appointment times, too, so if there is a little lay over, you can introduce your 9am to your 10am, and maybe they can be of value to each other.

"I can do that," I thought. And I did! I picked out my favorite bookstore/coffee shop (slash wine bar, mmmm wine), in Central Phoenix (Hello Changing Hands!), and started booking appointments every Wednesday.

I made it a point to work on business from the bookstore from about 7am-4pm each Wednesday, and then I reached out to people on my contact list and asked if they had time to get together for a coffee or snack. To keep my energy, I also invited personal contacts, too-not just business contacts. This greatly enhanced the friendships I have and kept us connected when life would otherwise lead to more moments of saying, "It's been too long."

Interestingly, my personal meetings actually led to as much business as my business meetings.

I think it is because the more you can move relationships offline, the faster you can really get to know each other. And, I truly believe that we are surrounded by people who love and support us. When we put ourselves out in the "arena," all of the universe, conspires to make stuff happen for us.

WHAT TO TALK ABOUT?

This was the first question I asked myself- Even if I do finally get the nerve to sit down with people, even my friends, what the hell are we supposed to talk about for 30 minutes to an hour...at a coffee shop?

I don't do small talk. I don't do complaining about life. I don't do drama. I don't watch TV (except for Golden Girls and some GOT), so I can't talk pop culture.

So, how can I guide a conversation that will get deep and fulfilling without being the awkward deep guy that *only* talks about deep and uncomfortable stuff?

Here's what I decided:

"Hey Susie, I see you bouncing all over the country on social media, having so much fun. Tell me what's new..." After a brief conversation, I always say, *"How can I support you in that?"*

No matter the intro, I always asked, what they are up to, and how I can support them. That changed the entire flow of conversation, deflecting the need for me to ramble on and on about myself and how awesome my business is.

At the end of the conversation, I've learned more about the person than I ever did, and I know exactly how to support them...sometimes.

The interesting thing I've learned is that many people do not know yet how they need or want to be supported. So, I just stay in touch, and I ask the same question, maybe in a different way, each time I see them.

Even though the other person has done most of the talking, sharing about themselves and what they are up to, we both feel connected on a different level. This has led to so many referrals, some of them instantly.

WHAT NOT TO TALK ABOUT

What not to talk about? Well, there are lots of things! For starters, avoid the habit of small talk for too long. You don't want to come to the end of your time together and wonder what this was all for. Hopefully you guys will part ways feeling inspired, invigorated, or at the very least, *heard*.

This is not a "kiki." Avoid falling into gossip and drama, either personally or professionally. The talk doesn't always have to be upbeat and positive, as your guest may be going through something intense, but you don't have to engage in the unhealthy side of that.

You. Don't talk about you...too much. It's weird how this works. Most people who are networking-averse resist even starting to talk about themselves. But then, when they finally do start talking about themselves or their business, they throw-up their features and benefits all over people, ignoring all social cues that the listener has checked out of the conversation. Ten minutes later, the guest is checking their watch, making up appointments they have to get to...now.

Don't be that guy (or gal).

When appropriate, share your business, and the passion you have for it authentically. Don't share it to get this person's business. Don't sell them on anything. Just be excited for your business. Enthusiasm attracts friends. If they're interested, they'll ask to be a part of what is happening or they'll know someone. Or, they won't...yet. But they'll remember your enthusiasm forever.

NETWORKING EVENTS

Whether we like it or not, finding the right networking event can be extremely beneficial for a mobile notary and loan signing agent. In a business where one person can change everything, networking meetings are worth their weight in gold...when you find the right fit.

One of the most popular networking meetings across the country is BNI (Business Networking International). This an extremely structured and organized meeting with chapters all over the US. In fact, most major cities have quite a few chapters.

One of the things I enjoy about BNI is that they limit the number of people from each industry they let in to each chapter. So, there is usually just one real estate agent, one mortgage broker, one escrow officer, one insurance agent...and one mobile notary. How cool is that?

In fact, that's one thing you can count on in a BNI meeting-there is *always* a loan officer, a real estate agent, and an escrow rep. Not to mention countless other business owners and attorneys, etc. BNI works if you work it, so it attracts a lot of top performers.

You'll also find that the mobile notary slot is almost *always* open. Very rarely will a mobile notary and loan signing agent make the commitment to show up and attend a weekly BNI meeting. It's time to raise the bar! Whether you choose BNI, or something similar, these events are literally rooms full of your ideal customers.

You can find all kinds of networking groups in your area on MeetUp.com. You can also find other notary meet ups there and start expanding your network of colleagues.

PEER NETWORKING & NOTARY MEET UPS

Working as a solo-preneur can get lonely. Plus, you can't be in two places at once, so you might appreciate having some notary colleagues to refer business to. You may enjoy some referral business from others as well.

You don't have to work completely alone in this business. There are many great notaries out there who love to share wisdom and resources to help you be better. Connect with those people. They will inspire and motivate you, and they can help you succeed. Even better, you may help them succeed, too.

As you grow your business, it will be important for you to be a resource to your potential clients. Even if you can't help them with that particular transaction, if you are able to refer them to someone in your network, they will remember you.

Networking is a skill to be developed, too. If you are not good at it yet, that's okay. Teach yourself through great books, a coach, or YouTube. Check the reading list after this chapter for a few of my favorites.

Check out the website for "MeetUp" for a comprehensive list of business networking groups in your area or even groups for notaries. You will find all kinds of different niche groups in there. Some of them are free, some charge a small fee to participate.

If you can't find the group you are looking for, you may be the one to start it!

Remember that meeting people and networking aren't necessarily for making cold calls to sell stuff. You're building relationships. These take time. And people work with whom they like. Meetings like this, and networking events or conferences and workshops, are where people decide if they like you or not. Show up and shine.

CONFERENCES & WORKSHOPS

In the spirit of Kaizen (Constant, Continuous, Improvement), I encourage you to stay on top of your game and raise the bar for notary performance in this industry. This will require that you stay on top of new laws, advances in technology, and more.

In some states, you can find some kind of notary or industry workshop, training, or conference. For other states, you may have to travel to a national level conference.

Stay in touch with major associations like The National Notary Association and the American Society of Notaries. They usually have events throughout the year.

Your Secretary of State, the office that *usually* governs notaries, will also be a great resource for state-specific trainings and workshops.

In California, the Notary Symposium holds two events per year in different parts of the state.

Get dialed in and stay connected. What I have found in this business, is that *you* have to be the one who makes the effort to learn more and be more. No one is pounding down the door to make you a better notary. Own it!

PERSONAL DEVELOPMENT SEMINARS

I mentioned earlier that all the marketing knowledge in the world will do no good if you have a personality that just turns people away. Sometimes, we don't even see it. These are our blind spots. When it comes to human interaction, we want as few blind spots as possible. We need people on our team. We need people to enroll in our dream, whatever it may be.

To do that, we need to work on ourselves-to lead by example.

Personal Development seminars, workshops, and courses, help us figure ourselves out. We don't know, what we don't know, so exposing ourselves to different teachings, perspectives, and strategies can save us.

This "work" is hard and not always pretty. That's why many people do not do it. However, if you want to elevate your experience here on earth, in life, and in business, take yourself on. It's worth it.

Try starting with anything Brendon Burchard. He's the leading personal development coach right now, and he has an enormous digital footprint with tons of free content on Youtube, Instagram, and Facebook.

Any event like this that you go to is going to be filled with people who are likely performing well in their industry, and they are looking for a way to breakthrough to the next level. These are people you want to be aligned with in business, too.

While at personal development events, the work we do on ourselves is critically important, and, it's important to be aware that you are surrounded by people who may be, or they may know, your ideal clients.

FAB 100 LIST

When I first realized that Escrow Officers were willing to pay me $150 to make sure some documents got signed correctly, I knew I had to make this explode.

Here I was, a fledgling entrepreneur, stretched thin with no money or energy, and no college degree. In any other field, there was no way anyone (in their right mind) was going to pay me $150 bucks an hour.

So, I opened my eyes and started looking for others who may need my services. More than that, I looked for people and organizations that had a presence in the media or the neighborhood that suggested they were *killing it* in their field.

I was looking at billboards, new subdivisions, newspapers (we had a lot more of them then), and the Business Journal's Book of Lists. That book literally ranks the highest performing companies in many different industries.

I started to put together my Fab 100 List. This was a list of companies and organizations that I was *not* yet connected with but *wanted* to be connected with.

These were real estate agents with lots of signage or closings. These were home builders that were building new subdivisions around my home. These were title companies I found in the Book of Lists. These were lenders or even individual loan officers that I saw advertisements for across my city.

It was not hard to get that list to 100 people. It's even easier now, with the strides of search engines and articles that rank pretty much anything these days. And, the physical location of a corporate office doesn't matter so much anymore. *Lots* of companies may be based in one state and do *lots* of work in yours.

When you make your own Fab 100 List, you do not have to "qualify" people and organizations before you put them on there. If they have caught your eye for some reason, put them on the list. We will research later.

I used an Excel spreadsheet for my Fab 100 (after a legal pad proved unworthy). If at all possible, include the name of the company, an individual who works there, a website address, email address, physical address, and maybe even a phone number. Definitely leave a column for notes!

You will not always have access to all of that info at first, and that is okay. Sometimes, all you get is a name, and that is okay, too. We are going to turn into little investigators later on in this process, anyway.

The key difference between this Fab 100 List, and your normal contact list, is that those on the Fab 100 List are not personally known by you …yet.

I know there are some pretty incredible CRM tools out there now, so if you can add a category or label these contacts as Fab 100, or whatever name you choose to call them, feel free to incorporate them into your database that way. There is no rule or reason that these have to be two completely separate lists. You do, however, want to know which contacts you actually know, and those you do not know.

To get started on your own Fab 100 List:

Open up Excel or Google Sheets and start a new spreadsheet.

Name it *Fab 100* or whatever you want to call it.

Name your first seven columns: Name, Company Name, Website, Email Address, Physical Address, Phone Number, and Notes.

Then, start looking for companies or people you want to do business with. You may have a few of them in mind already because you see their faces on signs and billboards all over the place.

Or you may have to Google, "Top 20 Real Estate Agents in _____ (Whatever city you are in-and neighboring cities!)." Or, Top 50 Escrow/Title Companies Near Me (or Closing Attorneys if in Attorney States).

If you live in a Metropolitan area with a Business Journal, they may have their recent "Book of Lists" available for purchase, too. This was the best investment I made when I first started out.

RESEARCH YOUR FAB 100

Now that you have a list, or hopefully at least a partial list, we can begin to dive a little deeper and do some research about who these people and companies are. Then we get to determine if we really do want to work with them or not.

This is where my strategy really begins to diverge from some of the other trainings out there. I do not believe you should work with just anyone just because you are desperate for work. You might think there is a certain reality to that. But let me offer you this perspective: if you are so desperate for clients that you would work with complete jerks, or people with values not aligned with yours, then you aren't ready for Escrow Direct business.

Stick with signing companies until one or both of these critical accounts reach the right level; it's either your bank account, or your confidence account. When these accounts are "low," you are willing to put up working with people who treat you, or others, poorly.

By doing a little work on the front end here, we can find out a *lot* about the people we are thinking about pursuing. We'll be able to tell, at least on the surface, if they'll be a good fit for us or not. Likewise, we may be able to tell if we will enjoy bringing value to them and their organization as well.

What we are doing is creating kind of a dossier on our potential clients, so we have some information about who they are and how they operate. We are going to use this information later on to connect with them on a deeper, more authentic level.

There are many areas you can go to find out information about people these days. Here are a few places to get you started:

- Facebook
- LinkedIn
- Instagram
- Google
- Better Business Bureau
- Chamber of Commerce
- Glass Door

Here are some things we are looking for as we research each company or organization:

- Who they work for (if individual).
- Who works for them (if company).
- Community involvement.
- Philanthropy/Charitable Giving.
- Recreational Sports Activities.
- Recent Promotions.
- Recent Speaking Engagements.
- Recent Family Additions (kids).
- Pet Announcements.
- Weddings, and other celebrations.
- Recent Travels, work or pleasure.
- Workshops, seminars, books they've read.
- Any obvious alignments they have with other companies (partnerships, etc).
- Religious affiliations.
- Alumni information.
- Courses enrolled in.
- Customer/client reviews.
- And also want to keep our eyes out for complaints and legal matters.

Do you relate to anything you've seen? Make a note in the notes section of anything that jumps out to you, especially if you can somehow relate to them, even on a personal level.

Did you go to the same university? Go to the same church? Do you play in a recreational softball league, too?

Everything matters, and you do not need to go through these with a fine-tooth comb. All we are looking for, on this initial go-round, are the people who really jump out at us.

In your research, try to fill in all 7 columns for each client with lots of notes about what you've found in your research. As a habit, I research 1-10 of these each and every day.

Let's look at an example escrow officer, Brenda Sample.

Brenda works for ABC Title company, and after Googling her name, we can see she has a Linkedin Profile, a Facebook Profile, and she just recently spoke at her local Chamber of Commerce, encouraging women entrepreneurs to invest wisely in their early years. In fact, she shared a recorded version of her presentation on her social media.

From her LinkedIn profile, we can see she attended and graduated UCLA with a BA in Liberal Arts, she volunteers at a no-kill animal shelter in her city, and she founded a youth leadership camp several years ago.

Her Facebook profile is open and public, so we see pictures of her family, with high-school-age children, and lots of RV trips to the mountains. It's also quite obvious she has dogs of her own, based on photos and the other Facebook pages she has liked.

She has a solid core group of Facebook friends that "Like" and tag her in funny memes and photos, so she appears to be social, well-liked, and friendly.

That gives us a *lot* of information about Brenda, and this is really only three sources; Google, LinkedIn, and Facebook. We'll now use this information in the next section.

If you come across someone you do not want to do business with, for any reason, I still recommend you keep them on the list, just so you have a record of it. That way you don't go through the trouble of researching them again down the road. I highlight anyone I decide not to work with in red on the spreadsheet.

On that same note, when I feel a real kindred connection to someone already, I'll highlight them in yellow.

Now that we have a little data to work with, let's connect with them.

AUTHENTIC AND CREATIVE CONNECTION

Believe it or not, finding closing agents is the easy part. Connecting with them, authentically, is where most new signing agents flounder a bit.

Let's define what it is we are trying to do here.

We obviously want to connect with our ideal customers. In this case, it's closing agents, whether that be Escrow Officers or closing attorneys. While we are definitely in business and have a service to provide, our goal is to connect on a slightly deeper level. The reason being, we need to separate our message from the rest of the dozens, or hundreds, of messages these closing agents get throughout the day.

Most mobile notaries and loan signing agents make the mistake of talking about themselves, more like provide a dissertation, of themselves and their services, when they are trying to market to closing agents.

Think of it like a date. If you talk about yourself, and how great you are the whole time, without regard or interest in the other person, your first date will probably be your last date.

This is where our research really comes in handy. We get a chance to talk about *them* first. And our goal is merely connection, not sales of our services.

For this reason, there is not a template email to send out to people. I do not do templates. Templates do not work when you're connecting on *a unique and authentic level.*

Let's go back and look at our example, Brenda Sample, and see what we can glean. We are looking for ways that we may personally relate to her and her situation. Take your mobile notary and loan signing agent hat off for a moment, and just be a regular human being. If you were looking for a friend, what about Brenda jumps out at you?

Let's break down each section of information we found:

Brenda works for ABC Title company. After googling her name, we can see she has a Linkedin Profile, a Facebook Profile, and she just recently spoke at her local Chamber of Commerce, encouraging women entrepreneurs to invest wisely in their early years. In fact, she shared a recorded version of her presentation on her social media.

From Google, we could ascertain:

- Brenda's role at ABC Title (There is likely going to be a title after her name and in her profile). In this case, for this example, she's an Escrow Officer.
- She's active on Social Media.

- She cares about people, and in particular, helping women plan for their future.
- We have access to a video that shows Brenda in action, so we can hear her voice, watch her mannerisms, and see some of her personality.
- She's not shy about the work she does. In fact, because she shared it, she may be proud of it.

From her LinkedIn profile, we can see she attended and graduated UCLA with a BA in Liberal Arts, she volunteers at a no-kill animal shelter in her city, and she founded a youth leadership camp several years ago.

From Linkedin, we can ascertain that Brenda:

- Lived in Southern California at some point (UCLA).
- She MAY be interested in the arts.
- She loves to help animals.
- She loves to help kids.

Her Facebook profile is open and public, so we see pictures of her family, with high school age children, and lots of RV trips to the mountains. It's also quite obvious she has dogs of her own, based on photos and the other Facebook pages she has liked.

She has a solid core group of Facebook friends that Like and tag her in funny memes and photos, so she appears to be social, well-liked, and friendly.

From Facebook, we may ascertain:

- She has a family life she enjoys.
- She has teenage children.
- They own or rent an RV and actually use it.
- She has pets and cares enough to like pet ownership pages.
- She has a sense of humor.
- She has friends.

Is there is anything about Brenda that you instantly relate to? Do you have a passion for helping animals or kids, too? Are you a woman entrepreneur? Are you a man who appreciates empowered women? Are you a member of a Chamber of Commerce? Do you have an RV? Or do you have a dream of owning one? Have you lived in Southern California, too?

For me, I have been a longtime proponent of youth leadership and empowerment and have been involved with a few organizations that help facilitate that. There's my connection!

Now, I may dive a little deeper and learn more about the youth leadership camp Brenda founded. Where is it? What's the website? What do they do there? Once I have more of an understanding (thanks to Google), here's what I might say in a quick email to Brenda:

Hi Brenda,

Wow! I just happened across your youth leadership camp, "Yaya Kids Camp," and I am so touched, moved, and inspired, by the work you do there. I am a lifelong advocate for youth, embracing leadership and empowerment on all levels. I know it takes a lot to get these programs funded and rolling. Thank you for the work you do securing and empowering our future leaders!

At Your Service,

Bill Soroka

Mobile Notary AZ

555-555-5555

Book a Notary

www.MobileNotaryAz.com

My email signature is the same all the time, and it has all of my company information in it. There is no need for me to "sell" anything here. I am a professional reaching out in genuine interest and admiration for Brenda. Her work matters, and I am acknowledging that.

You may have related more to the animals that Brenda works so hard to protect. Start there with a very similar message. Here are some rules of thumb to keep in mind:

- Resist the urge to sell your services in the first couple of interactions.
- Keep your messaging short and succinct.
- Avoid trying to contact closing agents during the last week of the month.
- This same strategy works when you want to call (on a phone), do an office pop-in, email, or snail-mail campaign. Do your research

upfront and talk about something more interesting than you and your business.

Whichever way you choose to approach Brenda, she may reply, she may not. Regardless, we're going to schedule a follow up.

THE FORTUNE IS IN THE FOLLOW UP

Here's what's real; your first contact with a closing agent is just that-first contact. Going back to our dating analogy, this is us sending them a "you're cute" or "I like you" note in junior high. First contact is *not* where you ask for their hand in marriage. First comes love, *then* comes marriage, then comes baby in the baby carriage…

After we send our creative, unique, and authentic initial message, we want to be sure we stay in touch. For some closing agents, this may be easier than others. Some closing agents, depending on your message, may respond right away, and ask you questions, or express gratitude. Let the conversation flow naturally, and *don't sell*…yet.

Remember, we are still laying the foundation of our relationship, and looking for ways to add value to this person. They already know what we do for work. Remember, our information was in our email signature line.

FIRST FOLLOW UP

Depending on how the initial interaction went, I'll look to schedule first follow up within 3-5 days. I'll look for a reason to reach out and connect. This follow up connection may be based on something I've seen on social media because I follow them. Or, more likely, I've happened across an article or book I think may be of interest to them. I want to add value to their work or personal life.

Here are a few "go-to" topics that may be of interest to busy closing agents:

- Stress relief (Escrow is one of the most stressful jobs in America).
- Eating healthier…at your desk (For real). Almost every closing agent I know is on some type of diet.
- New notary laws. Almost every closing agent is likely a notary already, but they're disconnected from the notary community. New info can be very helpful to them!
- Specific articles about what you've learned about them in your research. For example, Brenda may appreciate information about the

RV road trip that chases 72 degree weather across the country. She may enjoy an article about How to Start a No-Kill Animal Shelter, too.

Whenever you choose to follow up, I recommend putting it on your calendar, so you do not forget. If you're doing this right, you will have *lots* of new contacts, and it will be easy to forget both following up, *and* what to say when you do. Use your calendar and the notes section!

You can also use Customer Relationship Management (CRM) software systems like the free Hubspot program to help track of your contacts and automate follow up.

SECOND FOLLOW UP

Within a week of the first follow up, I'll reach out again. With this connection, I will get to either a live meeting on the calendar, if the timing is right, I will introduce them to someone who may need their services or may be able to help them grow their business.

One of the fastest ways to get your foot in the door, with anyone, is to introduce them to someone who will "buy" from them. In our case, closing agents are actively seeking connections to high performing real estate agents. That is *their* ideal customer.

So, if we can introduce our real estate agent friends, family, and colleagues to our escrow officer, Brenda, then that will get her attention real quick.

If I do not yet have a connection for Brenda, then I am going to ask to take her to lunch or buy her a coffee (whatever it may be to get some facetime). The faster you can take an online relationship "offline," the stronger that relationship will be.

Here's what that email may look like:

Hello again, Brenda!

I've loved that we have connected over the last two weeks. It's so important to me to support like-minded professionals who work so hard to make a difference in the world. I would love to take you to lunch so I can learn how to best support you in your business. Are you available Thursday at 11:00am?

Bill

ASKING FOR REFERRALS

Up until now, we have really focused on how to warm up "cold" contacts. Now, let's focus a bit on how to cultivate your current network. In today's world, there is a really good chance you already know people who work in real estate. These are typically real estate agent or loan officers. Do you know one or a few?

As you gain experience and venture into working escrow direct, your very own network may be the key to your success.

Any high performing real estate agent or loan officer will have their favorite closing agent. And, they probably have two or three of them!

You see, technically, borrowers get to decide where they want to open escrow for real estate transactions, whether it be a refinance or a purchase. However, most consumers are relatively unfamiliar with where to go and why, so they rely on their expert real estate agent's and loan officer's advice to guide them.

These experts will likely have at least one favorite closing agent, and a back-up, and then a back-up for their back-up.

So, what does that conversation look like?

Here's the strategy that worked so well for me that I actually stopped using it because I got too many referrals.

Here's a conversation I had with my friend, Shane, a loan officer:

Bill: "Hey Shane, I see you hustlin' and posting such great work for your clients all the time. I am happy for you-Congratulations!"

Shane: "Thanks Bill! Looks like you're killin' it too!"

Bill: "Yeah, I am loving this mobile notary gig. It's blowin' up more than I ever thought possible! Speaking of which, I am always looking for great escrow officers to work with. Who is your favorite escrow officer?"

Shane: "Oh man, I have three that are amazing! Maria at Fidelity, Paul at Pioneer, and Imelda at Mirage."

Bill: "Three favorites!!! I love it! What makes them your favorites?"

Shane: "Maria is OCD and has perfect files that close on time with, no questions asked. Paul takes great care of my clients and has one of those personalities they just love. Imelda has been in the business for over 30 years and if I have a wonky file, she gets it done!"

Bill: "Oh man, these are exactly the kinds of people I want to work with. Would you mind introducing me via email, or with a meeting?"

Shane: "I'll do an email intro right now on all three of them! Hope it works out!"

This is a dream connection. The key is to get the introduction. Just getting a name or an email address or just a business card, won't cut it. That still may work, don't get me wrong. But an introduction via email or in person, will far surpass.

Imagine it, this real estate agent or lender client of an escrow officer, sends an email that says, "Hey, I think you two should meet or chat." There's a little bit of an obligation to at least open up the door for you. There's no guarantee that you'll get the closing agent's business, but you'll likely get a chance to connect.

Couple this connection, this "foot in the door," with a little bit of research, and you may have a huge win!

BE READY FOR YES!

Many notaries spend months preparing for this business. They build relationships, spend money on certifications, training, supplies, and equipment. Then, when their phone starts ringing and dinging, they're still *not ready.*

Business happens when it happens. It doesn't always work around your shower schedule.

And signing companies and closing agents have hundreds of tasks per day, so if you aren't at the ready and prepared to take business when it comes, they are moving on to the next person.

Whether you choose to believe it or not, you are likely surrounded by people who want to support you in your success. Sometimes all you have to do is ask. Once you do ask, sometimes it is like the flood gates open and you get all kinds of referrals and opportunities.

Or, if you take this advice seriously, and start implementing these Daily Do's, things are going to start happening for you. And it happens faster than you expect, and when you least expect it.

You need to be ready for it.

HERE ARE SIX WAYS YOU CAN BE READY FOR "YES:"

- Establish and maintain a consistent digital presence.
- Answer your phone, texts, and emails professionally.
- Have your office set up.
- Wake up, Dress Up.
- Provide more service than you are paid for.
- Get training or instruction for skills you need.

MAINTAIN A DIGITAL PRESENCE

We live in a digital age, and if you want to be successful in this business, you will need to represent yourself and your business well on the web.
What does that look like? Well, it can mean a lot of things, but here are a few things to consider:

WEBSITE

You should have a website, no matter what. Here's the thing, if you are only going to be a loan signing agent, with no interest in growing a general notary work wing of your business, you can keep your website super simple-like one page simple. You just want to have some information about you, why you are passionate about this business, and the value you bring. You can even point a domain name to your Linkedin Profile, a business Facebook Page, or even your SigningAgent.com profile. The reason this can be so simple is because the people who hire you, closing agents and signing companies, will rarely use search engines to find a signing agent. They use directories and referrals! A website just gives you a chance to show value and provide contact information.

If you plan on building a general notary work (GNW) business, you need to go deeper, with a more comprehensive website. Most importantly, you will want access to be able to Search Engine Optimize (SEO) your site. This is a skill all to itself! Still, a necessary one. The reason being, your potential GNW customers are jumping on to Google and Bing looking for a "Notary Near Me." It is imperative that your website show up on the first page of Google to keep your phone ringing and dinging.

ANSWER YOUR PHONE

All the marketing in the world will do no good if you don't answer your phone, your texts, and your emails, in a timely manner, *and* with a professional and friendly tone.

I have signings that occur in all 50 states. Before I had a course that created an *incredible* community of qualified and friendly signing agents, I would have to find notaries on databases, like SigningAgent.com, 123Notary, and NotaryCafe.

It amazes me how many phone numbers I have to dial before I find someone who actually picks up the phone. Or, at the very least, just has a voicemail message that even hinted that they are still in business.

Even further, if I did leave a message or send a text, 95% never even returned my message.

If you are going to use this business to be of service or use it as a vehicle to put your dreams in motion, step up to business leadership and answer the call.

Maybe you can't take the appointment. Maybe you're not ready. Maybe you still have to work a day job. Maybe you're sick.

That's okay.

Answering the call, helping when you can, politely declining, *or* even better, being a resource to put the client in touch with someone who *can* help them, is leadership.

Demonstrate that in your business, and you will be unstoppable.

Consider using a professional voicemail message on your phone. Something like, *"Thank you for calling Mobile Notary AZ. I am likely at an appointment with a client right now, but I'd love to chat with you. Please leave me a voicemail and I will return your call as soon as I am done. Often for a faster response, you can also text me at this same phone number. Thank you for calling and I look Foreword to being of service!"*

If you want to take that to the next level, consider changing that message up every single day with the date included. *"Thank you for calling Mobile Notary AZ, today is Tuesday, November 2 at I am likely in an appointment…"*

WAKE UP, DRESS UP

You've probably heard, "Dress for Success" at some point in your career or lifetime.

It's one of those clichés that just happen to ring true, especially for mobile notaries and loan signing agents like us.

We are most often solo-preneurs, working alone and on a schedule that could, quite literally, change minute by minute.

People need a notary *when they need a notary.*

Potential clients may be members of the public for general notary work. They may also be closing agents, like escrow officers or attorneys, who have a client that needs us.

Most signers aren't too interested in working around *our* schedule. It's the other way around.

I love it when I get a week's notice of a signing coming up, or even at least a 24-hour heads up.

But it doesn't happen like that.

Sometimes, a borrower has been put through the grinder on their path to homeownership or refinance, and at the last minute, underwriting throws some additional stipulations at them.

Once those stipulations are met, often at the last minute, the loan is good to close.

A loan might clear underwriting at 10:00am, docs might be sent to title by 11:00am, title is going to call the borrower and find out their availability. The borrower is catching a flight to D.C. for work at 4:00pm that day. He can sign at 1:00pm only. Title is calling you with less than two hours until the signing and they still haven't prepared their end of the documents.

And…

It's an hour drive for you to the borrower's location. There's no time to "get ready." You have to wake up, dress up, and be ready for yes.

Business moves at a fast pace. Don't get left behind.

Even if you have zero appointments on the calendar when you start your day, you could end your day having 6-10 appointments.

That's how fast things can change.

And there is no time for you to jump off the couch, shower, coordinate a babysitter, find all your notary stuff, print or pick up documents and make it to the appointment on time.

It doesn't have to be that stressful.

Wake up. Dress Up. Work your business like you are clocked in because… you are.

OFFICE SET UP

As a mobile notary and loan signing agent, our offices are often at home and in the car. This requires a certain amount of organization, so we don't go absolutely crazy.

When I first started in this business, I had no idea what I was doing. I used Word invoice templates and had an archaic system of folders spread across my desk, indicating who had paid, and who had not.

I had a pile of printers in my office that probably worked, had I put some time into it. I am not a tech guy, so when they stopped working right, I'd buy a new one.

I ran out of pens all the time.

I ran out of stamp ink all the time.

It was unnecessarily stressful.

If you are just starting out, or even up and running after a few years (like I was), take a little time and get your sh*t together. Your peace of mind is worth it.

HERE ARE FEW THINGS TO HAVE IN MIND:

- Have a way to print.
- Have a back-up print option.
- Be sure to have both legal and letter size paper on hand.
- Keep all of your notary supplies in one place-like a bag.
- Keep pens (both blue and black ink) in great supply.
- Keep your vehicle well-maintained and fueled up.
- Have a way to create, send, and track invoices for payment.
- Make sure you have a working smartphone.
- If you have kids, parents, or pets that require caretaking, have a plan and a backup plan for this way ahead of time.
- If you are doing General Notary Work, you'll want a way to process credit cards.
- Also for GNW, you will want a way to give a receipt, even for cash transactions.

- Those are just a few of the ways you can prepare yourself for business. The more processes you can systemize and automate, the easier your business will be, and the more peace of mind you will enjoy.

PROVIDE MORE VALUE THAN YOU ARE PAID FOR

Several years ago, I made the decision that I was going to start picking up loan document packages direct from my escrow officer clients, as opposed to downloading and printing them.

This did a few things.

First, to my clients, it looked like a much higher level of customer service.

Second, it kept me front and center in the minds of *every* escrow officer in those buildings. This got me countless extra signings because I was always in the right place at the right time.

Third, because I was in the office so much, I could really focus on building deeper connection with my clients. This greatly enhanced the strength of the relationships.

Fourth, my printing expenses were cut by ⅔.

In addition to picking up the documents, I made a commitment to drop the fully executed documents off to the escrow officer *immediately* following the appointment. This meant I had to build a little more time into my schedule, and drive many miles out of my way, but it ultimately paid off.

When my clients began to see how fast I returned documents, their trust in the process increased. They could now send me out to do same-day closings, knowing that I would get the docs back in plenty of time to fund and record that day.

That prompted my client to then offer me even more fee per signing. They were saving a small fortune on courier and shipping fees, even within the same city, because the other "big" notary company they were using did not offer same day document return. They insisted on FedExing, even from one side of the Valley to another.

That was my value. My niche.

That boosted my signing fees by $50-$150 more per appointment, depending on the location.

Add to that my willingness to do signings anywhere and anytime...I had made my mark.

It took me a bit to "train" my clients to get them to believe that when I said, "anytime," I meant it. I built a name for myself as a crazy notary that welcomed 4:00am, 5:00am, 11:00pm signings.

Once my clients knew I was serious, they started offering those times to their customers. That meant more business for me. A lot more.

There are many ways to bring value to this business. Find the way that works for you. Even if it doesn't seem profitable from the get-go, you might find a little niche.

This industry is ripe for innovation. You just might be the game-changer.

Deliver more value than you are paid for. That's the biggest secret.

ADVERTISING YOUR LOAN SIGNING SERVICES

When it comes to more traditional advertising for your loan signing services, there is very little you will need to do. Closing agents, our ideal customers, do not find us all willy-nilly on the internet or in magazines. They use the directories we talked about earlier, signing services/companies, or they work directly with you after you've worked to build a relationship with them.

This means you won't have to pay for billboards, commercials, magazine ads, etc. Still, there are a few things you may want to have in place for spreading the word about your business.

Please note, I am talking about advertising your loan signing services only here. If you are promoting general notary work, that's a whole other story. I'll have a brief section on general notary work at the end of this book.

BUSINESS CARDS

Of all the marketing pieces you will use, a good old-fashioned business card will get the most use. People still ask for these when you mention what you do for a living.

WHAT TO INCLUDE ON YOUR BUSINESS CARD

Naturally, you are free to get as creative as you want on your business card, but historically, simplicity rules. A few things every business card should have on it:

- Your full name (What people should call you)
- Your title (Mobile Notary and Loan Signing Agent, Notary Signing Agent, whatever you decide)
- Phone number (the one you will answer professionally)
- Email address (preferably a professional one, not your @aol.com- See Phase 5)
- Your web address
- Your USP- Optional (In marketing, this is your Universal Selling Proposition-tag line, Your Value, what sets you apart)

WHERE TO DESIGN & PRINT YOUR BUSINESS CARDS

There are a *ton* of great resources for us to design and print our own business cards. I use Canva's free templates to design my card. I then download my creation from Canva and upload the design to VistaPrint for printing. This is a very affordable option.

Through years of being in business, I've learned some things about me. Because I like variety and I change my mind about domain names and phone numbers, I only buy 100 or so business cards at a time. That way, if I do change my mind, there is less waste. It costs a few bucks more, without the bulk discount, but it's worth it to me to have some flexibility.

SOCIAL MEDIA STRATEGY

I could probably write an entire book on just social media strategy. Luckily, plenty have come before me to do just that.

There are all kinds of social media options these days. I recommend choosing a platform you are familiar and comfortable with. If it is Facebook, start a Facebook business page for free. If it is LinkedIn, dress up your profile professionally and represent your new business.

If you are social media averse, I recommend stepping out of your comfort zone and choosing one platform to get to know. You are in business now.

Also, keep your professional image in mind at all times. Remember that as a business person, people are deciding whether or not they want to do business with you based on your online behavior. Choose wisely.

Across the platforms, there are some general guidelines I can suggest.

SHARE THE JOURNEY

There's nothing more annoying than someone, or some corporation, that does nothing but advertise their products and services on social media. That's not what we go there for. While research is still being developed on what really drives us to social media, I would wager it is not to be sold to…constantly.

For most of us, we want to feel connected, to be a part of something, to get informed, entertained, or distracted. We want value.

Give us value, then!

In a relationship-based business, like this mobile notary and loan signing agent gig, people work with whom they like, admire, and respect.

If you're out hustling, making stuff happen, driving across the city to help your customers, share the journey with your audience.

I am not talking about sharing personal information about your clients, or an over-abundance of selfies (nothing wrong with selfies, by the way! People respond *very* well to them).

Take photos of mountains, animals, coffee mugs, pens, cars, freeways, whatever it is in your day-to-day that is somewhat interesting and demonstrates your passion for what you do.

When it comes down to it, that's what we want to convey- the passion and joy we have for what we do every day. *That* attracts people! *That* attracts our ideal customers!

I started sharing my travels around the city on both my personal Facebook feed and my business pages, and it really helped establish my reputation as a mobile notary and loan signing agent that *loved* the road.

I started getting tagged in posts and photos by friends when some of their friends would post looking for a notary. Now it happens *all* the time! Not everyone understands exactly what I do, but they know three things:

1. I am a notary
2. I *love* what I do
3. I'll go just about anywhere to do it

As part of my Daily Do's in Morning Mastery, I committed to posting at least once per day on the social media platforms. This could be a blog article or just a picture with something interesting about the people, pets, or pests I met along the way.

There really is no such thing as over-posting these days-if you are doing this right. Sharing the journey, whether in business or in personal life, is really what social media is all about. It's when you keep posting advertisements for your business that this can get old really quick for your audience.

It's totally okay to drop a nice graphic ad, or a "If you ever need a notary, call me," every now and again, but they should be rare in comparison to sharing the journey and providing value.

For me, the most profitable strategy I ever used on social media was offering *free* notary services to friends and family. In fact, that was the *only* time I ever advertised my services-and that was maybe once or twice per month. The rest of the time, I shared my journey, my passion, and my personality.

To reiterate- my most profitable campaign was offering *free* notary services! By offering services for free, my posts got shared more, my friends remembered me, and I got *tons* of referrals. And, to this day, I don't think I have ever done a free notary service for friends. They all insist on paying me, one way or the other-tips, wine, or food. Plus, they send me to all of their friends and family for notary work.

LINKEDIN STRATEGY

What if there was this place where closing agents, loan officers, and real estate agents all gathered and shared a *lot* of information about themselves? What if they even made it easy to contact them?

Well folks, that place exists, and it is called LinkedIn.

LinkedIn was one of those social media platforms I was aware of, and I even had a pretty mediocre profile I used, mainly as a digital resume. I had some vague notion that it was valuable in business, but I really never dove deep enough to figure it out, until recently.

Doing what I do, I read a book that suggested I read Sandra Long's book, "LinkedIn for Personal Branding." I read and implemented many of the strategies in Sandra's book, and saw an increase in profile views. Plus, I learned a lot, which I love.

Still, I wanted more, so I went back to the book, and implemented some more strategies on dressing up my profile. I wanted to be proud to send people to my LinkedIn page. As I read through the book even more, it was clear that LinkedIn was *the* resource I would need to find and connect to Escrow Officers.

They were all right there, at my fingertips. Along with their assistants, and even their bosses. LinkedIn was a goldmine.

I decided to reach out to the author, Sandra Long, and invite her to present a webinar on how notaries could leverage LinkedIn as the ultimate resource in growing their business. The timing was perfect! Sandra was so cool, and we immediately set up a webinar, which you can find on the resource page.

More than that though, Sandra was in the middle of creating her own course that teaches anyone on how to optimize LinkedIn. She calls it LinkedIn Personal Best Sales Club and you can get 20% off by going to the link on the resource page. The course took my LinkedIn presence to an entirely new level!

Here are some basic tenants to take away for your LinkedIn strategy:

LINKEDIN PROFILE

- Spend time on this- it matters and represents your entire brand.
- Show some personality and passion in your summary.
- Always use a clear, professional quality photo in your profile.
- Include all aspects of your life and history, like education, volunteerism, work, business, etc.
- People will find you on LinkedIn through a search *or* when you are referred.

NETWORKING AND COMMUNITY

- Be strategic about who you connect with.
- Be professional and personal in your communication.
- Understand the different levels of connection on LinkedIn.
- Know how to search for people, organizations, or roles (titles)- this is *huge*!
- Learn how to leverage LinkedIn Messaging, Invitations, and Groups.

- You don't have to be a creator of content to be visible. Consider commenting and sharing.
- Use Hashtags and Mentions.
- Keep yourself "top of mind" for your clients.
- Know what types of posts you should be doing?
- Create articles and posts on LinkedIn to establish authority and branding.
- Visibility = Opportunity!

I learned all of this, and so much more in Sandra's LinkedIn Personal Best Sales Club course. If you want to improve your LinkedIn and social media skills, schedule some time with this every day or at least every week.

SKILL DEVELOPMENT

It's impossible for us to have *all* the skills needed for success without learning them. We were not born knowing how to run a successful business or how to negotiate contracts. We have to grow into, or become, good business-people. That takes experience and learning.

For most of us, we graduated high school or college and then stopped learning. If we read at all, we read nothing but fiction books that, while interesting, don't necessarily help our personal development.

As business owners, in a relationship-based business, we *must* again prioritize our learning processes. We have to schedule our learning, just like we did in grade school. I make this part of my morning routine. Then I also schedule about 30 minutes of intentional learning around noon.

How do you know what to learn? Since you are starting your business, this is a little more obvious, right? You need to learn how to become a notary, learn the notary laws of your state, learn how to get certified as a loan signing agent, and learn how to do the actual work, like describing the documents, etc. Then, you have to learn where to find your ideal customers and how to connect with them. And finally, you have to learn how to manage your business on a day to day basis.

That's the big picture- the five big steps to becoming a mobile notary and loan signing agent:

1. Become a Notary Public.

2. Get Certified as a Loan Signing Agent.
3. Documents, Processes, and Etiquette.
4. Business and Personal Development.
5. Management and Resources.

Look familiar? That is the general lay out of this book *and* the Sign & Thrive Notary Training Course and Community. Anytime we have a big goal or dream, it helps its attainability if we break it down into five big steps.

Once we have these five big steps, we can fill in all the gaps-the little steps that go into each of the five big steps. Much of these little steps will be the learning, growing, and becoming we will need to experience in order to accomplish each big step. This is why they say "success is a journey, not a destination. Goals are not about their attainment, but more about who you become as you accomplish them. There is a lot of growing that has to happen!

So, here we are on Big Step Four on your path to becoming a six-figure mobile notary and loan signing agent. We've already discussed several skill-sets you will want to learn, maybe even master, on this journey. Here are a few more for you to consider. Keep in mind, that this is not a rush job. For many of you, just the content of this book, or the course, is going to be your skill building for a while. That's okay! Study the material, hone your craft, and launch.

But, never stop learning. Forever be the student. This business is your masterpiece and will require a commitment to constant evolution.

There is an epidemic in our industry that I call the "50 Signing Princess." New loan signing agents come in, excited and enthusiastic to learn the business, absorbing knowledge and coaching, eager to do well. Then, as they gain momentum, and their confidence soars, somewhere around their 50th signing, they think they know everything and check out of learning.

I know signing agents with 20 years of experience who still don't, and will never even pretend to, know everything. In fact, I know escrow officers with over 30 years of experience that still do not know everything about everything. The most successful of them are never afraid to ask, and always go to new trainings, required or not.

Forever Be the Student.

That's how you set yourself apart.

Now, for those ideas on things you may want to study. Create your own "life curriculum."

POWER OF PRESENCE

Being present for yourself and others is one of the keys to building relationships. Have you ever had a conversation with someone and you were quite sure that it didn't really matter if you were there or not? They would have just kept talking or found another face to talk at?

In loan signings and notary appointments, this shows up for us as stress over the documents, worrying about our next (or last) appointment, traffic, making it to FedEx before the cut off, and more.

The more we reign this in and learn how to focus our attention on the present moment, and the present client, the more successful we can be.

Show up for your client 100% of the time.

The book and teacher that kicked this whole thing off for me was Eckhart Tolle's *The Power of Now*. It's a deep read and an even deeper practice that has the power to change your life.

PUBLIC SPEAKING

I know this is one of the number one fears of people. You may never actually step up in front of a room full of people, but public speaking skills can still benefit you as a mobile notary and loan signing agent.

Whether for networking meetings, notary meet ups, trainings, or even just one on one signing appointments, being comfortable when you are speaking to, or in front of others, will serve you well. If you want a little taste of what this is like, check out Toastmasters International. You can often visit a few times, at no charge, and just get a feel for what their program is all about.

Dustin Hogan, founder of the Rockstar Academy, created a free public speaking masterclass for mobile notaries and loan signing agents. You can watch the replay on the resources page.

SEO

Search Engine Optimization is a skill that will serve you well when you have a website that you want to rank on page one of search engines. This is how customers find you! SEO is a dynamic, ever-changing industry, and also quite expensive to outsource. Build SEO into your learning and take your time with it.

We'll talk a little more about SEO in Phase 5.

What else do you want to learn about? Or, maybe I should ask, what *should* you learn about to reach the levels of success you're dreaming about?

PHASE 5-
MANAGING YOUR DAY TO DAY BUSINESS

"Entrepreneurship is living a few years of your life like most people won't so you can spend the rest of your life like most people can't."

—Warren G. Tracy's student

INTRODUCTION

There are a myriad of resources for notaries of all levels that will help you manage your day-to-day business. I am going to share some that I use myself and I'll share what other notaries across the country are using. The truth is, I am a creature of habit, especially when it comes to technology. So, in some cases, I have been using the same systems from the beginning, even when I know there are better ways out there.

In those cases, I will share with you what my students and collaborators around the country use.

There are many, many resources here for your use in managing your business. If you need it, you can likely trust there is an app for that. If there isn't an app or a service for it yet, then maybe you can invent it. This industry is *ripe* for innovation.

IMPORTANCE OF SYSTEMS

Whatever tools and resources you end up using, focus on building systems that make your life and business run smooth and efficient. It doesn't matter if you manually create invoices or hire a virtual assistant to do them on Quickbooks for you-just systemize your processes and free your mind and desk of clutter.

I *love* the practice of writing, by hand, on a whiteboard, giant post-it, or in my journal. That is how I process things and remember them. I have handwritten notes for everything. Many of my client contact lists, the original Fab 100 List, and even some of my first invoices were done by hand.

There is no pressure to run out and drop thousands of dollars on all of these products and services, especially in the very beginning. There are some critical pieces you'll need, and I'll be sure to make clear what those are. The rest, you can grow into as you generate revenue or prioritize them.

TOOLS OF THE TRADE

Let's start at the beginning, in Phase 1, where you become a Notary Public in your state. There are certain supplies you will need to perform your function. Some states can differ and have specific requirements, so again, you'll want to confirm with your state statutes or even the Secretary of State (or governing body).

NOTARY SEAL (OR STAMP)

In nearly all states, a notary must have a seal, otherwise just known as their stamp, to use for notarizing of documents. The content of the notary seal can also vary by state. A typical notary seal/stamp requires:

- Name of the notary.
- Commission number.
- State and maybe the county of commission.
- Commission expiration date.

Luckily, if you order your stamp from a vendor familiar with the process, they'll know what you need. The National Notary Association can be a great resource for purchasing bundled packages with everything you need.

In fact, my friend and colleague, Laura Biewer, offers free personal concierge service to help navigate the process and customize packages with the NNA. Feel free to find her contact information on this book's resource page and ask her for free assistance with the NNA products and services.

NOTARY RECORD/JOURNAL

Journals are cheap and easy to come by. In fact, some states actually allow you to make your own, if you follow guidelines. Still, you can buy decent journals online for around $10, so splurge, and buy yourself something nice. Just be sure to check your state statute to make sure you are using a journal that complies with local laws.

For me, I actually spend twice as much as I need to on my journal, around $20, at my local UPS Store. I try to support them as much as possible to help build a relationship. Then, if, and when, I ever need their support, they have my back. And, you'll be surprised how helpful it is to have a print shop *and* shipping company on your side when you need them most.

OTHER TYPES OF STAMPS

In the course of their work, notaries may have occasion to use other types of stamps that will make their work more efficient. Here are a few examples of what those may look like.

EMBOSSER SEAL

As a kid, I used to love using my grandfather's embosser. The way it crimped the paper and left an "official seal" just triggered the deep (not that deep, I guess) inner nerd in me. An embosser creates that raised seal impression on paperwork that many of us associate with a notary in the first place. The reality is though, we rarely use this type of seal. In most states, it will *not* be necessary to purchase this. In fact, if you are doing loan signings, lenders do not want you to use an embosser.

That said, there are some industries that may even require an embosser. So, if you plan on pursuing general notary work, you may consider purchasing one.

JURAT/ACKNOWLEDGEMENT STAMP

You won't find a huge need for these types of stamps in loan signings, but it can still be so useful if you are in a state that allows their use.

These stamps contain the verbiage that essentially turns any document into an acknowledgement or jurat, as you need them. These come in super handy with handwritten letters, or typed documents from the public. This is a must have for general notary work!

CALIFORNIA DISCLOSURE STAMP

In California, and a couple other states, notary Acknowledgments and jurats must have specific language about the role the notary plays and does not play. There are stamps available to easily add this verbiage to any document. If you are in California, or any other state that requires the disclosure, you'll definitely want to have this stamp.

FORMING YOUR BUSINESS

CHOOSING A NAME

Choosing the name of my businesses was always the fun part for me. Especially, when I was dreaming big. What would be my next *big* thing? I used to spend hours, sometimes weeks, picking the perfect name that history would remember.

Well, as a mobile notary and loan signing agent, we are not likely to be running TV commercials and building global brands, so hiring brand managers and spending weeks on choosing a name isn't necessary.

In fact, changing your name in this business has proven relatively easy, too. Nothing is permanent. Since so much of your business is based on you and your personality, no matter what you name your business, your clients are working with you, *because* of you.

This point struck me when I went through one of many name changes at a point when I was *killing it* in business. I hired a marketing firm to create this beautiful logo, a new website, and some other promotional material.

I sent out emails to my clients, letting them know that my company name was changing. Did it matter? Nope. They still just called me Bill Soroka, the Notary. When they really got to know me, they just called me Billy.

My brand name didn't matter to them. I *was* the brand.

So, to most of my clients, I am just William Soroka, Notary Public. Short and simple. That's who they make the checks out to. Behind the scenes, I have a business entity set up, and we will talk more about that in a second.

For now, there are some points to consider when you choose your business name.

TO USE YOUR NAME OR NOT

Like William Soroka, Notary Public, you could choose to keep it simple like that. You can even go with Smith Mobile Notary, or another way to tie your first or last name into it.

GEOGRAPHY

Some people would rather use cities, states, or landmarks in their name. Something like Chicago Mobile Notary or Grand Canyon State Notary, etc. Later when we talk about Search Engine Optimization you'll see the value of this.

KEYWORDS

Keywords are those popular words that describe our services that consumers might be typing into search engines in order to find us. An example of this would be "24-Hour Mobile Notary," or "Friendly Notary".

SIMPLICITY

Don't over-complicate this. Remember, we are not necessarily building a global brand as an individual mobile notary and loan signing agent. Sure, we may have dreams of scaling this thing to a major national signing company, but we don't have to choose that name right this instant.

If you have your scalable brand name in your head, go for it! But, don't let the name choice bog you down. Just choose a name that is simple and easy to remember.

Also, you want to be sure your name is actually available to use. My first test for this is whether or not the domain name is available for a website. A domain name is like your address on the internet, like www.SmithMobileNotary.com. We are going to go a little deeper with domain names in the next section.

I use www.GoDaddy.com for all my domain management. You can go there and search your chosen name (even if it is just your own name) and see if it is available. If it is not available, I go back to the drawing board on a name, because this domain address is how most of your customers will find you.

If the domain name is available, I then search my state's business name directory to see if it is available for registration as a DBA or organization as a business entity (more on this later). This business directory is usually available on line with your state's Secretary of State.

REGISTERING YOUR NAME

When you wish to do business under a name other than you own, you have a few options. In fact, in some states, counties, and cities, you may have some requirements. Even if not required for operating your business from a legal perspective, some banks may have rules for opening accounts for businesses where you use a different name.

When you operate your business using a name other than your own, or even other than your legal business name, this is called your DBA (Doing Business As).

Registering a DBA is relatively cheap and easy, no matter what state you are in. This is typically done with the Secretary of State, or Corporations Commission.

Registering your DBA can help in some ways, and it is severely lacking in asset protection and full business organization, too. You may want to get some tax and legal advice as you progress. I'll talk about a few of your other options coming up here pretty quick.

BUSINESS LICENSE REQUIREMENTS

In some states, counties, and cities, becoming a commissioned Notary Public is enough to begin transacting business. In others, you may have to get a business license. The best resources are your state's tax authority, Corporations Commission, or Secretary of State to find out what is expected of you. You can always contact a tax and legal expert for advice as well.

BUSINESS ENTITY

You've probably heard of the four main types of business entities: Corporation, S-Corporation, Limited Liability Company (LLC), and Sole Proprietor. There are even Limited Liability Partnerships (LLP) for qualifying professions.

As a mobile notary and loan signing agent, you'll need to decide the best entity for you. To do so, you really should consult a legal and tax professional to get the best advice for *your* situation. If you simply Google this, you'll get so many answers from armchair experts that your head will spin. It can be overwhelming. In fact, this is where many new notaries hit analysis paralysis and just freeze.

I am not an attorney or tax advisor, so I am not offering legal or tax advice here. I would like to help add some clarity to general situations, so you don't let this stop you from taking action.

First, let's clear something up- formally organizing your business as a corporation, LLC, S-Corp, or Partnership is typically *not* a requirement to transact business. In fact, most mobile notaries and loan signing agents operate as a sole proprietor.

Second, formally organizing your business does *not* legitimize your business to your customers. They don't care how you've set up your business behind the scenes.

These formal business entities are mainly designed to do two things: Protect Assets and Improve Tax Efficiency. That's it.

As long as you are compliant with state, county, and city guidelines, you'll likely be able to launch your business as a sole proprietor, as so many notaries before you have done. Then, as your revenue increases, it may make sense to organize your business differently. Get some tax and legal advice at that point and make the appropriate changes.

Now, if you have significant personal assets you wish to protect, or if you anticipate significant revenue in your first year, get the advice you need in the beginning. If this is the case, you already know the value of a good advisor.

Here's what I did:

I operated as a sole proprietor, using only my name-William Soroka, Notary Public, for the first few years. Then, as revenue increased, and I could afford better advise, I organized as an LLC. As an LLC, my tax advisor made some suggestions (like paying myself as an employee), implemented some changes, and filed taxes as an S-Corporation, minimizing self-employment taxes.

Again, I am not a tax advisor and do not know your situation. Use my scenario as talking points for your own conversation with your own tax and legal professional.

FILING TAXES AS A MOBILE NOTARY AND LOAN SIGNING AGENT

When it comes to filing your taxes, the Federal, state, county, and city laws all vary. So, I have to advise you to check locally so you are in compliance with your laws.

That said, I can tell you that some states actually do not count your Notary Public Fees as income (state level only), so be sure to check into that. And at the very least, your actual fees for notary service may not count as income for self-employment and tax consideration.

The way you file and pay taxes will depend a lot on what you've decided to do with the section before this. Which entity did you choose?

Finally, some jurisdictions require payment of estimated taxes each quarter, so again, get yourself a tax professional who can help navigate this.

A good tax professional will understand the tax deductions a mobile notary can take as well. Be thinking of things like, training, paper, printers, fuel, vehicle maintenance, mileage, pens, clothing, meals, and more!

MACGYVER NOTARY TIP

Be sure to read IRS Publication 334 about Notary Public income and the possibility it can be exempt from self-employment tax. It is critically important to get expert tax advise on whether or not it is wise for you to take advantage of this ruling or not. There is a link to the publication on the resources page.

YOUR DIGITAL FOOTPRINT

I am going to give you a real quick run-down of the digital expectations for a mobile notary and loan signing agent. Remember, most notaries will not do most of this. This is *your* greatest opportunity. Consider these a "best practice."

Still, if these are not in your wheelhouse of expertise, or if they are not in your start-up budget, don't stress too much. This can all be incorporated as you grow.

DOMAIN NAME

As I mentioned earlier in this section, when I choose a business or brand name for myself, I do a domain name check first before I make a final decision.

Your domain name is your address on the web. It is how people will find you. When you choose a domain name, there are a few things to keep in mind.

Easy to Remember- Do your customers (and you) a favor and choose a domain name that is easy to remember.

Keep it at three words or less- For example, www.SmithMobileNotary.com would work out just fine. You have three relevant words. What you want to avoid are things like, www.BillJohnsonMobileNotaryPublicTallahasseeFlorida.com

— That won't work because no one, including you, will remember it. And, it probably won't event fit on your business card.

Get the .com- There are all kinds of extensions available. You can get a .com, .org, .co, .net, etc, but nothing else matters if you don't get the .com. Why is that? Because consumers are still trained to go to .com for *everything*.

As an example, let's say you want to buy www.SmithMobileNotary.com, but someone else owns it. They don't have a website or anything on it yet, but they own the domain and they don't want to sell it to you.

You think, ah, no big deal, I'll just buy www.SmithMobileNotary.*net*. You're thinking you might be kind of crafty and sly, but this might end up biting you in the rear end. Even though we tell people *.net*, they will inevitably type *.com*. That's how we are trained. Then, all of your marketing may end up helping whomever owns that .com name.

If you can't get the .com, keep looking. That's your best practice.

And, that said, we aren't building a clothing or real estate empire here, so if you *really* love the name you came up with but can only get the .net or the .org, go for it. You know the risks. Make your decision.

When it comes to domain hunting, I favor GoDaddy. They usually have a .99 cent promotion for first time clients, and even without that, domains are around $15 per year.

YOUR DOMAIN NAME IS NOT YOUR WEBSITE

If you're relatively new to technology and the web, it's easy to confuse your domain name (your address) with your website. If the domain name is the address, then your website is your "house." You must build it, or, pay someone else to build it. Just having an address does not mean you have a house. You may just have an empty lot.

Now that we have beat that address and house analogy to death, let's talk about whether or not you even need a website, and what your options are for building a website if you do.

DO YOU NEED A WEBSITE?

As an independent loan signing agent, having a website will not likely have a significant impact on generating more business for you. "Why," you ask? Let's think back to Phase 4 on how loan signings are generated for you. It's one of three ways- through relationships that you establish through your efforts; Signing Services/Companies; or random calls from Closing Agents that have found you on a directory.

Most Closing Agents and Signing Services are *not* going to random search engines and searching for a loan signing agent. They are going to trusted resources and directories that already ensure we are criminally background checked and certified. That's why as an independent loan signing agent, a website will not necessarily be a revenue source for you.

That said, I still recommend it.

Even if you're going to be an independent loan signing agent, a website can help enhance your brand. While a Closing Agent may find you on a directory, they may also do their research on you to see if you're someone they want to work with. Having a website, and social media profiles, that show engagement, professionalism, and some personality, *can* help you land a deal every now and again. In a business where one connection or relationship can change everything, this is worth it.

Aside from that brand control, another great reason to have a website is for business expansion beyond your loan signing services. The focus of this book is loan signing, so I won't spend a lot of time on multiple streams of income. Just know there are many to choose from, including General Notary Work (all the other stuff notaries do). A website can be your central hub for sharing your services-all of them. Check out the Side-Hustle Lounge appendix for some more ideas.

WHERE TO GET A WEBSITE

There are so many options available for getting a website. I'll give you a couple of ideas and resources here, and then you may be able to find something on your own, too. Here's what I want you to keep in mind for your search:

1. Always maintain control and access of your website or at least have access to make your own changes. This is critically important, because if you have to rely on someone else to make changes or additions to your website, you're then working on *their* timeline and

that doesn't always align with yours. I have seen relationships crumble in these situations.

2. Own your brand! Spend the fifteen bucks and actually buy a domain that reflects your name and/or brand. Avoid using free website services that do not allow you to use your own domain name. The last thing you want is a domain that says www.wix.smithmobilenotary.com. You're advertising for Wix, not you.

With those two things in mind, here are a few options for building a website:

1. Hire someone else to do it. For a basic website that we would need, this could run anywhere from $300-$1,000 depending on the designer. If you have a friend who will do it for "free," just remember the two points above.
2. Build Your own using template services like GoDaddy's Website Builder. These "drag and drop" templates can really make web design easy and fun.
3. I've partnered with Green Monkey Marketing to design a series of notary specific templates that are available to you for free ($750 value) with the purchase of a web hosting package at Green Monkey. This will run you somewhere around $330 per year for hosting and give you access to support, training, and a world class website. You can check it out on the resources page for this book.
4. Google has some incredible resources available for small businesses, like us. Among them, the "Google My Business" suite of marketing services that can help put your business on the map. Using Google Pages, you can create a basic website completely free of charge on your own.

WHAT CONTENT SHOULD BE ON YOUR WEBSITE?

When it comes to the kind of information you want on your website, the sky is the limit, and every expert will have their own opinion. It can be very overwhelming! Still, in our industry, there are some guidelines to keep in mind.

1. Always stay compliant with state laws for Notaries Public, and the SPW Code of Conduct. Each state can be different, of course, but some require that it includes a fee schedule and/or certain disclosures. Your state statutes or notary handbook will be the best resource for this. SPW stands for "Signing Professionals Workshop," and was a group of industry professionals who got

together a few years ago and established a Code of Conduct for signing agents to work by. The Loan Signing Agent Certification Exam offered by the National Notary Association (Phase 2) is based on this Code of Conduct.

2. Make your homepage more about your customer and their needs than about you. Think about the state of mind when a customer finds your website. No one really needs a notary until they need a notary. They don't want to read your family history and why you love this business before they can find out if you can help them. If you want to dive deeper into yourself, your family, what lead you to this business, and why you love it, do so on an "About" page. I also highly encourage you to do that! Many people (myself included) make buying decisions based on the personality and passion a person shares with me.

3. Make contact information clear and prominent. If your customer has to hunt for your phone number or email address, you'll lose them. Please avoid using the classic "Contact" page as the *only* way to get ahold of you. Your phone number or email address should be all over your website. It's totally okay to have a contact page, too, but you need a phone number and/or email address on every single page, at least, once.

4. Be sure your site is "Mobile Friendly." Research shows that 56% - 74% of web searches are done on mobile devices. There is a *very* high likelihood of your customers being on a smartphone when they are looking for you. Most template website companies already include this feature. You'll want to be sure you test it out and make sure the order of words and images match up on the mobile version of your website.

5. Make a different page for each of your services. As I mentioned before, there are *lots* of ways to add services and value that will increase revenue streams. If you decide to go this route, create a separate page for each of these services. For example, if you offer Loan Signing Services, and General Notary Work, have a page for each. If you decide to be a Wedding Officiant, too, make a separate page for that service. Sell pre-paid legal services? Make a separate page for that, too.

DON'T EXPECT "BUILD IT AND THEY WILL COME"

We've established that having a website is important, for brand control, displaying your array of services, and possibly even lead generation (especially for general notary work). Many people make the mistake of spending time, energy, and money, building a fabulous website, and then passively sit back and wait for the phone to ring.

At the time of this publication, there are nearly **two billion** active websites on the internet. Two Billion. The expectation that we can just build a website and hope that one of the approximately 200 million adults over 18 in the United States are going to find us just isn't realistic. The odds get worse when we consider the amount of adults over 18 within our working radius, as mobile notaries and loan signing agents, that just happen to stumble across our website.

In order to make sure your website is found by *local* customers who need your services *when* they need those services, you've got to be *actively* working your website. This work happens behind the scenes and requires consistent attention and activity. The process is called Search Engine Optimization.

SEARCH ENGINE OPTIMIZATION

Search Engine Optimization (SEO) are all the actions and processes we can take to increase the amount of, and quality of, the web traffic to our websites through organic search engine results. Basically, this means everything we do to help our websites show up on that coveted page one of Google, Bing, or Yahoo, so our customers can find us when they need us most.

SEO is dynamic and changing all the time. If search engines change their algorithms, the whole industry can flip over night. There are entire companies that do only SEO for clients. They get paid to stay on top of the industry, helping their clients get the competitive advantage for everything from TV's to gym memberships. And I might add, they're compensated quite handsomely, too. In many cases, working with a quality SEO firm can cost around $2,000...per month. SEO is an ongoing expense!

Quality SEO can take time, when you do it correctly. This is a significant expense for the everyday mobile notary and loan signing agent. In fact, it really isn't a reality for many of us.

Instead, we will likely need to learn how to implement SEO on our own. This is one of those ongoing skill sets that I would *highly* recommend *if* you plan on pursuing general notary work in your endeavor. As a loan signing agent, as I mentioned above, this is of little consequence, and likely not worth the energy.

However, if you are one of the growing thousands of loan signing agents finally ready to embrace general notary work, having an SEO'd website will be critical to your *thriving success*.

PROFESSIONAL EMAIL

Having a professional email address is a simple and inexpensive way to show how serious you take your mobile notary and loan signing business. A professional email address usually includes your name @ your domain name. You see these for businesses all over the place and it really raises the bar of professionalism.

For example, john@smithnotary.com would work just fine. Or, if you want to keep it more general, you could use something similar to what I use in my business- orders@notarycoach.com.

At the very least, get an email address with a free service, like Gmail, that is dedicated to your business. That could be smithnotary@gmail.com. This is not ideal, but it is a good, free, work around for now.

Please be aware that your ideal clients, your prospects, will see your email address and make judgements about you based on it. They can't help it any more than we can. We are humans and we judge. Keep your email address professional and avoid things like:

Hotdad402@hotmail.com

SexyMama85012@msn.com

Isign4u@outlook.com

darlenesgranny@aol.com

These are cute and might do the trick getting business of a different kind, but these do *not* belong in your mobile notary and loan signing business.

On a side note, please avoid using AOL completely. The perception of AOL is that it is antiquated and used by those who are not technologically savvy. In this business, and any business that deals with people, perception is reality. I have seen escrow officers skip right over a notary because of their AOL email address.

I've used great companies to provide my professional email addresses. I currently use Google's G-Suite for business. It looks like Gmail so the learning curve was minimal. It runs $5-$10 per month. Prior to G-Suite, I used GoDaddy E-mail. Checkout your options and choose what you like.

OFFICE SETUP

Now that you have your basic tools of the trade and you have a little more insight as to your digital set up, let's look at your ideal office set up.

As a new mobile notary and loan signing agent, your "office" will likely be in your home, at least at first. I am going to share both necessities, and what might be considered "luxuries" for us as well. There is some equipment that isn't necessarily a requirement but makes life a lot easier for us.

Like many things in this business, you can scale up or down, depending on your needs and budget. Don't stress too much about these. There is almost always a work around to fit into any budget.

SMART PHONE

Believe it or not, you can run your entire business via smartphone these days. With the right technology, you can:

- Receive documents.
- Send for printing.
- Scan Documents.
- Answer emails, calls, and texts.
- Generate invoices.
- Send out thank you cards.
- Upload images.
- Navigate to Addresses.
- Do just about everything else you need to do with your business.

There does not seem to be any significant difference between Apple and Android phones in this business. Do what is comfortable for you. The last thing you want to throw at yourself when you're starting a new business is the learning curve of a new smartphone. You will be using this all day every day.

I am an Android user (no judgement). I use the Galaxy S9, and I have opted for the biggest screen possible since I am working on it all day long.

PHONE NUMBER

When it comes to the phone number you use for your business, you have a couple options.

You can just use your mobile phone number. This is the easiest on the front end, as it does not require any additional set-up and it's easy to remember (it's *your* phone number). The downside is that as your business grows, this mobile device will have to be attached to your hip at all times. A missed call is missed revenue.

The other option you have is using a phone number service, like Google Voice, that provides you a separate phone number that your customers can call. You can then Foreword that call to the number of your choice, like your own mobile number. There are lots of perks to systems like this, including custom voicemail messages that will be transcribed and emailed to you. Also, as you grow, you can Foreword the calls from your business to someone else on your team without having to give up your mobile phone.

While Google Voice is free, there are some paid services like, GoDaddy, Grasshopper, and E-Voice, that you can look into as well. Because you will be publishing your business phone number, this is one of those decisions you will want to make in the beginning phase of your business set up.

COMPUTER

As I mentioned earlier, just about everything I need to do for my business can be done via smartphone. Still, sometimes it is nice, and even necessary, to have more power, more storage, or a bigger screen to work with.

The main reason you'll want or need a computer is for the printing of your loan document packages. While it is possible to print direct from your smartphone these days, that requires a level of tech savviness that isn't for everyone.

If you're not a Steve Wozniak on a smartphone, then you will need a computer of some sort. There is likely no need to go out and buy a new or anything. Your same old computer or laptop *should* do the trick.

If you happen to be a person who does not own a laptop or computer right now, you can find Chromebooks, or similar, for around $200 and those should suffice.

PRINTER

Aside from your tools of the notary trade and your smartphone, your printer is likely the most important tool. As a loan signing agent, you'll be expected to print loan document packages that vary in length from one or two pages, to the average 150-200 pages.

As we discussed in Phase 3, these loan document packages are also comprised of both legal and letter size pages, so it will be important that your printer be able to handle the job. And, like so many other things in this business, there are options to fit nearly any budget. I am going to talk about the ideal printer situation to get you started, and then I'll share an alternative if your budget requires something different.

Home office printers can range between $30 and $2,000 and have a whole bunch of functions that you may, or may not, use for your mobile notary and loan signing business. Luckily, the ideal "work horse" printer that will get you started in this business will likely cost you around $300.

While I do not personally endorse any particular brand or specific printer, I will share some specifications you'll want to look for. In fact, I'll share the exact brand and model that many notaries swear by.

PRINTER SPECIFICATIONS

As you're looking for a printer, there are a few key specifications that will make your business run smooth and efficient. See the list below, as well as the explanation as to *why* these specifications can help.

USE A STAND ALONE (NOT ALL-IN-ONE) PRINTER

I know I'll get a lot of pushback on this, as "Printer-Pride" is a real thing, but I am not a fan of All-in-One printers. I think when you try to do everything for everyone, something suffers. Technology has proven this time and time again.

Some of these All-in-One printers have everything but the coffee machine attached (and that is probably on its way soon). I know Printer/Copier/Fax/Scanner/-it sounds like a great value. And, there may be many quality models out there that will disprove this recommendation. But in my experience, one or more of these functions jam up or fail, rendering the entire device worthless. Your peace of mind matters! If you're constantly fighting your printer, you will go crazy in this business. You use it way too much to have to battle every time.

Do you need a printer? Yes (Obvi!). Do you need a scanner? Yes, probably (more on that later). Do you need a copier? Maybe… Do you need a fax? What's a fax? (No, you don't likely need a fax machine, by the way).

Given that, I recommend the stand-alone printer that does what printers were built to do- print!

DUAL TRAY IS IDEAL

When they say "dual tray," they are referring to the fact that there are two drawers; one for the letter size paper, one for the legal size. This allows for printing both letter and legal-size documents in the order they are received. That may not be something you've thought about just yet. These loan packages do not just come to you all organized with all the letter sizes together and all the legal sizes together. They are intermixed, letter/legal, throughout the document…sometimes. Some packages are *all* letter size, too.

Get used to inconsistency. Every lender, every closing agent, and every signing company will have their own little ways of doing things. Some will make sense. Some won't. We get to navigate those details.

LASER OVER INKJET

When you're printing 150-300 pages (remember you have to print two copies sometimes), ink is a major consideration. Typically, Laser Jet printers are more efficient with ink, which will cost you less in the long run.

Also, Inkjets have been known to smudge. If the ink is smudged on critical documents, lenders and government agencies may reject the paperwork. That will result in you having to make an additional trip (possibly), and/or losing a great client.

BLACK & WHITE ONLY

A nice perk of the biz is that all loan documents are printed black and white only. This can help save on your ink cartridges, especially if you choose the right printer.

SINGLE-SIDED PRINTING ONLY

Loan packages have to be dissected and scanned/uploaded/emailed to various companies by the Closing Agent, so it is imperative that they be printed single-sided *only*. There have been many instances where new notaries attempt to save paper (money) by printing front and back for these loan packages. This backfires and they find themselves out of business very quickly.

These novice printing errors are hard for signing companies and escrow officers to forgive, so just don't do it.

PRINT SPEED

As technology has evolved, it seems like this is less a consideration these days, but I would be remiss in not mentioning it. As mobile notaries and loan signing agents, we often receive documents at the very last minute, or even late. If we have a slow printer, this could make things worse for us and our customers. A good print speed is around 40-45 pages per minute (or faster).

YOUR STARTER PRINTER

Picking out a printer is so overwhelming! Google it and see what happens. Walk into Best Buy or Staples and browse the selection. How do you know what to buy? There are almost *too many* options!

I am a big believer in reviews, so that is usually where I start. But still, how do you know if one printer's functionality will fit with this? Start with what we know. Notaries before you have spoken.

As the founder of Notary Coach, and the Sign & Thrive Notary Training Course and Community, I get to speak to a *lot* of different notaries across the country. That gives me a lot of data, and I get to hear their preferences and experiences.

Hands down, the most recommended printer is the Brother HL-5200 and the HL-6200 dual tray printers. The dual tray feature is important because these are sold with single trays, too. The main difference between the two is the print speed-the 6200 is a little faster and around $80 more.

You should be able to find the 5200 for around $220-$250 on Amazon.

ALTERNATIVE TO DUAL TRAY PRINTER

So, what if your budget doesn't allow for a $300 printer purchase in the very beginning? I promised you there would be affordable options, so let's talk about that.

Page Separator is a software that will allow you to use just about any *single tray* printer you can find, as long it is capable of at least printing on both letter and legal-size paper. This will help you because single tray printers are significantly cheaper than dual tray printers.

When you upgrade to their Professional Edition (recommended), the software will print out all of the letter size documents at one time. Then, all the legal-size documents get printed. The Pro edition gives you a report that shares the stacking order of the documents, so you can reorganize them the way they should be.

Check out the software, and their explanation videos on our resource page.

BACK UP PRINTING OPTIONS

Before we talk about back up printing options, I'd like to remind you have the importance of privacy and information security. These loan document packages are packed full of very personal information that can be very valuable to the criminally minded.

As mobile notaries and loan signing agents, it is our responsibility to protect this information, while the documents are in our control.

That said, we also have to get business done and service our customers. And...things do not always go as planned. Printers don't always work. Appointments take longer than expected. Lenders and Closing Agents forget documents.

For peace of mind and for optimizing your client experience, you might consider having a back-up printing option.

If your budget allows, this might literally be having another dual tray printer in your home or office. You may even consider having a single tray printer with the page separator software ready to go.

Many mobile notary and loan signing agents have a portable printer equipped to work in their cars, too. These are not necessarily ideal for every print job you have, as these mobile printers have a tendency to work at their leisure. Because of the motion of the vehicle, and constant bumping around, sometimes the parts jimmy around on you. And, sometimes dust, dirt, and grime from the road can clog things up.

As a back-up or emergency plan B, these mobile printers may work for you.

If that is not an option, you can consider utilizing an outside printing source as a last resort. There are third party printers, like Office Max, UPS Stores, and local print shops that have self-serve printers available for use.

While we certainly do not want to make a standard practice out of this, having a back-up plan can help you get the job done when it is critically needed. Keeping information security in mind, there is some risk when you use an outside printer. There are some ways to mitigate this risk. If you choose to use this system, keep a few things in mind:

1. Be prepared to accept 100% responsibility. "The Buck Stops Here."
2. Choose a print shop that either does not store records (electronically) of the print jobs, or they at least delete the data daily. Just FYI, today's printers have a memory chip that "remembers" printed data. If someone can gain access to that data, they have your customers information. Therefore, it is imperative that the memory device has been removed or it gets wiped daily.
3. Choose self-serve options *only*. These documents are for your eyes only.

PRINTING CAN BE A PAIN IN THE A$$

When it comes to home printing, there are a lot of moving parts. And, I don't just mean the nuts and bolts of the physical printer. There are different software and operating systems that have to communicate in order for these loan document packages to print correctly. Sometimes it is as easy as clicking one box in your print options. Other times, it feels like the stars have to align in order for your loan document package to print.

I share this with you to prepare yourself a bit for some level of frustration. If you can't get your printer to operate the right way, you are not alone. In many cases, your PDF reader software, like Adobe, will have to communicate with your web browser, like Chrome. Chrome is trying to communicate with your computer's operating system, like (like a Mac or PC). Your operating system is trying to communicate with your physical printer. One little miscommunication can lead to hours of frustrating calls with tech support.

You do have resources available to you- Start with the manufacturer's tech support hotline (if they have it). Then try online forums for the manufacturer, or for notary support. Many of us have been through similar situations and *may* be able to help. You can also try The Geek Squad, or other tech support contractors like them.

SCANNERS

Picture it, you've just finished a 200-page signing and the closing agent requires you to scan back the critical docs listed on a checklist they provided.

It's about 70 pages worth of scanbacks (also called faxbacks). Your all-in-one printer has a maximum capacity of 15 pages. That's going to require 5 separate scans that will drive your closing agent client crazy. So, you'll either have to wait through 5 scans, and merge the PDFs so it all goes over as one convenient file, or send them 5 separate files.

I'll tell you now, the easier you can make your client's job and life, the better you will do in this business. It is far better to send the scanbacks over as one file.

That's where your separate scanner will come in handy. Some of these standalone scanners can get 50-100 pages in one scan. And many of these scanners are easy to transport, so it can be relatively easy to make them mobile, if you want to go down that road.

Stand-alone scanners can also be quite expensive, ranging from $200-$600 on Amazon and Best Buy. I found a high-quality Brother scanner at Costco for just under $300.

INEXPENSIVE ALTERNATIVES

There are several smartphone applications that can "scan" documents for you. Once you pay for (around $5 or so) and download the app, you can just use your phone's camera to take pictures of each document. The app converts the images to a PDF and whim, bam, boom, you have a file to scanback. It can take a few extra minutes to take individual photos of all those documents. But if this is what your budget calls for, you work with what you've got. You can always upgrade to a full scanner later on after you start generating revenue.

The scanner app I use and enjoy is called "TinyScanner." You'll want to upgrade to the pro version, so you can create a multiple page PDF. The cost is around $5.

PAPER

When it comes to the paper you use for printing documents, you can go with standard, inexpensive, copy paper. There is no need to upgrade to fancy paper for this. In fact, it is almost better you do not. Cases of paper are available all over the internet and in office supply stores, including major stores like Wal-Mart. Paper is one of your greatest expenses in this business, so it is worthwhile to hunt down and track good deals. Just remember, you will need both letter and legal sizes.

PENS

I am a pen freak! I love a good pen that makes writing even more enjoyable. I like to provide that service to my signers as well. If they're going to sign their name 200 times, why not make it the most comfortable experience as possible?

That's partly why I upgrade my signers experience with high quality pens. My new favorite pen right now is the Tul Medium. These cost around $1.25 each, which is a bit pricey for a pen you may lose at each signing. Do what is right for you and your budget.

My previous favorite pen, and still a great runner up, is the G2 pens from Pilot. These are a little more affordable.

And, there are no rules about the brand or type of pen to use (usually), so if you want to go with a standard Bic, you can do that too.

Where there will be rules for you to follow, is the color of the ink you use for loan signings. Most lenders will require everything be signed in blue ink. But, with that said, there are always exceptions to this. Some lenders will require black ink. It's best to stay stocked up and ready for both.

Always have lots of pens. Then have back up for your pens. Don't make the mistake of taking writing utensils for granted. Many of your signers will be in transition-moving from one home to another, at work, in the car, at a Starbucks- and pens will be in demand.

THANK YOU CARDS

One of the most powerful tools I have used to deepen relationships and grow my business have been greeting cards. Namely, thank you cards. A simple show of gratitude can go a long way, especially when you are authentic, and pure (not advertising) when you do it.

One of the secrets to be good at this is to look for reasons to be thankful for something. Sometimes this is easy, like when you get a signing from a closing agent or signing company. Other times, you may have to dig a little deeper.

I remember one time, as I was researching an escrow branch office, I saw that the Business Development Officer was very active with a community organization I valued. She had led an event that raised money for the organization and had been honored for her work. I sent her a card, thanking her for her services to the group. That relationship blossomed and eventually turned into a business partnership.

You can send "nice to meet you" cards, "Congratulations" cards, "condolences," and just about anything else you can think of to stay in touch, and just acknowledge the people you interact with.

Some notaries like to handwrite each card on their own. Others like to use technology. Again, this is one of those services that can be scaled to any budget. As you are first starting out, you might make your own cards and send them out.

As you progress, you may consider purchases pre-printed cards, or even buy custom cards. There are two great services that I used to help make sending cards fast and efficient.

Send Out Cards- Send Out Cards has a smartphone app that allows you to build a custom greeting card, using photos from your phone or from a database. You can even have the card printed in your very own handwriting font. Their factory in Utah then mails the greeting card to your recipient, and they receive it within about a week. I had a lot of luck with this! And, if you'll recall from my "post-signing" ritual in Phase 3, this is one of those things I do after every single signing.

Send Out Cards also has an income opportunity attached to it, where you can be a referral partner and earn commissions if other people purchase the product using your splash page. If this calls to you, it could be a nice revenue stream. If it does not appeal to you, don't stress, as you can be a customer only as well.

TouchNote- Touchnote is another service that works very similar to Send Out Cards. There is not an income opportunity attached to Touchnote. It is simply a smartphone app where you buy credits and then can use those credits to create and send greeting cards.

KEEPING TRACK OF YOUR CONTACTS

Recall from Phase 4 where we talked about how important your contact list can be for staying in touch with prospects, clients, friends, and family. Say it with me, "The fortune is in the follow up!"

Using a Customer Relationship Management (CRM) software or tool can make this a lot easier on you.

These CRM's will allow you to schedule follow up reminders and automate that contact. You can send emails, and even greeting cards, without even having to think about it.

The world's top sales professionals have some sort of system in place for this. These days, it is usually technology based. Even if you manually write reminders on a calendar, this still works. The most important thing about this is to have a system that you'll actually use.

When I first started out, I used a legal pad for my contact list. What can I say, I like to write! Doing this manually was powerful in the beginning because *it got me started.* I didn't have any excuses not to take out a pen and paper and start writing down names. Sometimes being intimidated by technology, or not understanding how to set up Excel, can impede your start. A legal pad and pen removes the hurdle. Just write down your Fab 100 list on paper. Who do you want to do business with?

If you are being effective in your hustle, a legal pad of names is not going to be scalable or sustainable for you. That list is going to grow quickly. Remember, you're supposed to be adding 3-5 names to that list every day-every damn day! At some point, you'll likely need to upgrade to either Excel, Google Sheets, or a CRM.

BOOKKEEPING

I have to literally pump myself up to talk about bookkeeping. Some people love this stuff. I am not one of them. Love it or not though, having a bookkeeping system is imperative for keeping your business running like a well-oiled machine.

Bookkeeping includes everything from creating and managing invoices, collecting payments, tracking your mileage, and cutting checks. This is a big category and I am going to do my best to share resources with you that will help you run smooth and efficient.

If you only take one thing away from this chapter, it should be this: *never* make your clients beg to pay you (Send your invoices on time). And, stay up on your accounting, no matter your system. Don't let invoices build up until the end of the day, the week, or the month. You won't get to them later. You will get buried underneath the pressure. Remember how important your peace of mind is! Take a few seconds each time an invoice is needed, or a check gets received, to document. Using technology can make this so easy!

INVOICES

If you've decided to go Escrow Direct for your signing business, there will be an expectation that you provide an invoice for your services *at the time your service is rendered.*

That means you should deliver an invoice for your signing fee with the documents when you drop them off. Sometimes this literally means printing the invoice and tucking it in with the signed copies before dropping or shipping them. More than likely though, it will mean emailing an invoice to the closing agent as soon as the signing is complete. Remember, those four things I do after every signing? Sending the invoice is one of them.

It can be extremely frustrating to a closing agent if they have to hunt you down and ask for an invoice, so they can pay you. Systemize your process with this so you can make your client's life easier!

Also keep in mind that every closing agent is subject to have their own system. Stay flexible! The last thing you want to do is require that your clients bend and adhere to your system. It really should be the other way around. Part of our role, and definitely part of our success, is to the extent in which we can make the closing agent's transaction go smooth and efficient.

WHAT TO INCLUDE ON AN INVOICE

As I mentioned, every client may be different here, but there are a few things you can likely count on for inclusion on a signing invoice:

1. Type of Service Provided (Refinance/Buyer/Seller/Cash).
2. Amount of Fee.
3. Date of Signing.
4. Borrower Last Name.
5. Escrow/File Number.

WHERE TO CREATE INVOICES

When I first started out as a loan signing agent, I had no idea I was even supposed to create invoices for each signing. I had no software to do so. I had no skills on how to make those look pretty either. My first escrow client, and friend of mine, just sent me an email that said, "Oh, hey, you forgot to send your invoice. Can you email that real quick? $150."

First, I had to pinch myself, because making $150 an hour was a pipe-dream two weeks before. After that I said, "Oh crap, how do I make an invoice?"

It wasn't like I started this business back in the dark ages or anything. But back then it was hard to find *affordable* resources for this kind of stuff. I ended up just downloading the basic, free template on Microsoft Word. I could type all the info I needed, save a copy, attach it to an email, and send over to my client.

Then, I would print the invoice out and put it into an "Unpaid" file folder. When I got a check in the mail a week or so later, I moved that paper invoice into a new "Paid" file folder. Talk about old school!

Still, I liked my system, and it worked…for a while.

Manual systems work fine until you get busy. They are not scalable, meaning they can't grow with you and your volume. If you don't switch gears and systems, you'll find yourself resenting your new volume because it causes you so much paperwork.

If you want to use a manual system like this as you get started, feel free. Your technological options are far greater today than they were for me. You can get smartphone apps and custom technology, specifically built for notaries, now, and it is affordable.

WHAT I CURRENTLY USE FOR INVOICES

Once I upgraded from my manual system, I found an online bookkeeping company that made the creation of invoices on the fly, in my car, super easy. That company has since been acquired by GoDaddy and is known as GoDaddy Online Bookkeeping.

The service costs about $15 a month and comes equipped with more reporting capability than I will ever use, but it really makes invoicing super easy. It also did not require a doctorate in accounting to figure out how to use it, which is important to me. I don't have a lot of time for the learning curve on technology like this. I would rather focus my energies on building marketing and relationship building skills.

CUSTOM NOTARY SOFTWARE

There are two software programs that have been created exclusively for mobile notaries and loan signing agents. These programs take into consideration the needs we have in documenting signing types, mileage tracking, special notes, and more. These can make invoicing super easy, and they even have a CRM component to them.

Pretty much everything we will talk about here in the Bookkeeping section can be managed through these two programs.

Check out NotaryAssist & Notary Gadget on the resource web page for this book.

INVOICING FOR SIGNING COMPANIES

When you do signings for signing companies, the invoicing system may change a bit. In fact, with many signing companies, you won't even have to send them an invoice. They'll have their own internal system for tracking your signings. Still, you should have a way of tracking your signings, too, so you can stay on top of your revenue.

When I still worked for signing companies, I used to generate invoices in my bookkeeping system, and then would *not* send them to anyone. This was so they'd still show up in my receivables, so I could tell what was paid and was unpaid.

Also keep in mind that some signing companies will still require you send an invoice, so be ready to adhere to their policy.

PAYMENT FOR SERVICES

Most of your payments for services will come from signing companies and closing agents in the form of checks or automatic deposits into your checking account.

As we discussed in Phase 3, the timing of your payment will depend on your client. If you are working "Escrow Direct," payment for services will look one of two ways, typically. You'll either be a line item on the Settlement Statement, which means you are paid upon closing of the loan (usually). The Closing Agent will just cut and mail you a check when they pay everyone else in the transaction.

If not a line item, you'll likely be paid from the closing agents general operating fund, or from their corporate office. You might still get a check for each individual signing, or they may ask you to "batch" your invoices once a week or once per month. I have had clients that are all over the board with their policies and preferences, so be ready to be flexible.

CREDIT CARD PROCESSING

As a loan signing agent, you won't likely be taking many credit card payments. Most of your clients are closing agents and signing companies that will prefer to pay by old fashioned check (or auto-deposit). Occasionally, you may have a lender or a real estate agent who will be covering the cost of your mobile signing services.

In those instances, I've found having a credit card payment option very handy for quick payment. These instances are few and far between. As you build relationships with real estate agents and mortgage lenders, they may actually start paying you with a credit card. It doesn't necessarily have to be a priority in the beginning.

Still, it is so easy to open a credit card processing account these days, so why not do it now? And if you plan on embracing general notary work, you *will* need a way to process credit cards, anyway.

Many of the accounting software programs out there have an add-on service, like Stripe, that makes a credit card payment option available on each of your invoices. Other services, like Square, make it simple and easy to start-up, too. Credit card processing today is not like it was back in the day. You don't have to set-up merchant accounts, wait for underwriting, prove assets, or buy expensive processing equipment. Check out your options! This may surprise you.

WHAT TO DO IF YOU DON'T GET PAID

In the course of your business, you may have a client that is either very slow to pay you or just doesn't pay you at all. There are many ways to handle this.

First, just know that you are a real business providing real services. You deserve to be paid for your work. That means, to the extent of the law in your state, you have every right to pursue a debt that is owed to you.

Second, you never really know what the story is behind the scenes or what people are going through. Give signing companies and closing agents the benefit of the doubt when you bring the unpaid invoice to their attention. Perhaps it was just an oversight, either on their part... or *yours*. Maybe they sent the check and you deposited it but forgot to mark it as "*paid*" in your system. I always start there:

"Hi Heather, I am so sorry to bug you with this, but I have this unpaid invoice from 45 days ago, and I just do not see a record of payment. You guys are always so prompt, so I am sure I just missed a check somewhere. Do you have a minute to look into this or put me in touch with accounting?"

An email like this should get the problem resolved. But, not always.

There are times when signing companies have to wait for their closing agent clients to pay them before they can pay you. Payments might take longer. Some signing companies communicate that better than others. So, your messages may get ignored, which adds fuel to your fire. Stay professional and kind. And keep reminding. Once per week until the 60-day point is more than enough (unless the company has a clear policy outlining a different expectation).

If your client is completely unresponsive, misleads you, or breaks promises to pay, you have every right to escalate. This doesn't really happen a lot, but it certainly can.

To escalate this, you can send a demand letter written by an attorney. These payment demand letters can be very effective, and very expensive when written by an attorney. I recommend a pre-paid legal service, like LegalShield, to help buffer the costs of these types of situations. I'll talk more on that a little later on.

In the worst-case scenario, you may just have to write off the loss on the invoice and chalk it up to experience. An invoice for $75-150 is not worth losing sleep or peace of mind over. Still, I think it is important for us to watch out for one another, too, not to mention, do our due diligence to mitigate risks like this.

In Phase 4, I mentioned Carrie Rivera's online community, Notary reviews. On Facebook, you can find her private group called *Notary Reviews: The Good, the Bad, and the Ugly* where she includes a list of over 500 signing companies that have been reviewed by your peers. There, you can do your due diligence to check the reputation of a signing company before you work for them. And you can also post a review based on your experience. I encourage you to post the positive reviews, as well as the negative ones. There are so many *great* signing companies out there!

RECEIPTS

Having a bookkeeping system that allows you to mark an invoice as *"paid"* will usually suffice for receipts as a loan signing agent. In fact, many closing agents won't even need the *"paid"* language on there. In order to close out their file, the checks have to be cut, so they know the invoice is paid, anyway.

Receipts may be requested or required for credit card payments or for general notary work. For credit card processing, like Stripe and Square, they have built-in receipt capabilities. You can text or email the receipt to your customer right away.

Just keep in mind that for general notary work, many of our transactions are paid in cash, and you may need a manual receipt book, too. Even when paying in cash, technology will still allow you to generate an electronic receipt-often through Square or your accounting software.

LEGAL SERVICES

I am used to starting businesses on a shoestring budget. And that budget rarely included paying $300-$400 an hour for a good attorney to set-up or advise my business entity set-up.

Still, in the course of my business career, I have had many needs for an attorney:

- Contract reviews.
- Employee disputes.
- Landlord/tenant issues.
- Non-payment of funds.
- Corporation dissolution.
- Business set-up.
- Insurance policy reviews.
- You name it!

The reality is, when you are out in the "arena," as Teddy Roosevelt called it, you are bound to run across people who treat you unjustly. You will need legal advice or representation at times. I spent the first half of my life only paying for an attorney when I needed one. It seems like no matter what the task was, it cost me around $1200 bucks. Some of those situations ended up costing me thousands of dollars, too!

Now, I'll spend the second half of my life with a sort of legal "insurance." Prepaid legal services allow regular folks like you and I to afford top grade legal services for around $1 a day. You'll pay a small monthly fee and will have access to world class legal services like:

- Contract Review.
- Legal Letters.
- Speeding Ticket Review.

- Business Entity Advice.
- Last Will & Testament Review.

Of course, certain restrictions apply, and I recommend you contact an independent representative to get the details for your state.

I am also an independent representative for one of these organizations and work with many other notaries on my team. Our professionals can help you out with the link on the resource page.

BANK ACCOUNTS

There are two schools of thought on setting up bank accounts for notaries. Some people advocate for having a separate business account for all revenue and expenses that pertain to your notary business. Others just prefer to use their personal accounts.

I prefer the former, and that is partially based on the opinion of my tax advisor. I keep my business expenses and revenue separate from my personal income. And by having a separate business checking account and debit card, I don't have to keep receipts anymore. Everything that runs through the business account is presumed to be a business expense (consult a tax advisor).

If you don't want an entirely separate checking account for your business, you may be able to accomplish similar results by using a designated credit card for *only* business expenses. Again, talk to a tax advisor who knows your situation and can help you set your business up efficiently.

MILEAGE TRACKING

For tax purposes, you may want to track your mileage for each signing. You may be able to deduct a portion of that. Also, for general notary work, many states actually allow you to charge for mileage, round trip, for each appointment. Check your state statutes or notary handbook for details.

To track your mileage, you can use an old-fashioned notebook, or you can use one of many different smartphone applications designed to do this. I use MileIQ and have been very happy with it. They offer a basic free version, and then it is around $5 a month if you go over a certain amount of trips.

Some of the bookkeeping software we talked about earlier will also have columns for adding and tracking your mileage.

YOUR SECOND OFFICE

If you've applied the principles of Phase 4, and you're hustling, then your phone will be ringin' and dingin'. That means you'll likely be on the road…a lot.

Your vehicle is going to be your second office, or in some cases, your second home- especially at the end of the month when it is traditionally busier than the rest of the month as a loan signing agent. When you spend so much time in your vehicle, and so much time on the road, there are some new, and maybe different, things you'll want to keep in mind and consider.

DO YOU NEED A VEHICLE?

As the "Share Economy" and the sustainable movement grow, I am asked more and more about whether or not having a vehicle is absolutely necessary to be successful as a loan signing agent.

I am an optimist, and I believe all things are possible, *and*, life without a vehicle as a loan signing agent would be very difficult. I am not saying you have to *own* a vehicle. You just need *access* to a vehicle.

Your signers are going to be every possible place a human being can get to- stores, coffee shops, campgrounds, mountain tops, jail cells, and more. You have very limited control over where these signings take place. Our service is designed as a convenience, so we have to be…convenient.

I would absolutely recommend having a private vehicle that you can access on demand. If that is not an option for you, there are no industry rules about how you get to an appointment, as long as you get there on time and professionally. You can utilize public transportation, rideshare (Uber/Lyft), your feet, a bike, a plane, whatever you can afford, right? At some point, your expenses may outweigh your income, and you do not want to work at a loss on every signing.

If you decide to do something that is physically straining, like riding a bike or walking long distances, please be prepared for ways to clean yourself up, before you knock on your signer's door. The last thing they want is a hot, sweaty, heavy breathing person on their doorstep. You represent an Escrow Officer or an Attorney. Act the part.

Another note about this: if you take alternative transportation, resist the need to share that information with the signer. You don't need to mention the bus, taxi cabs, or Uber to them. Take care of your business…privately. And *please* do not wait for transportation in front of your signer's home (unless safety is an issue). Step around the corner and wait where you can't be seen.

Taking public or alternative transportation can be perceived as unprofessional by some people. In a people business, perception is reality. If the signer says anything about a sweaty mess, awkward lingering, weird behavior, or taxi-cab riding, signing agents, you may very well lose a client. Remember, you are representing the closing agent! You are an extension of them, and their services.

TYPE OF VEHICLE

There are no "rules" about what kind of car you have to drive to do this job. Still, there are some guidelines and best practices to keep in mind. Regardless of your type of car, or how it looks, remember that even if *you* don't care about image, your client might. And since you are representing them at your signing appointments, it will serve you to be sensitive to that.

If you're toolin' around in a '77 Mercury Marquis Brougham like John Candy's character drove in the movie "Uncle Buck," with multi-colored fenders, dirt and grime an inch thick, and a consistent (and distinct) backfire that has your neighbors hittin' the deck every day, then you might want to park down the street a bit.

VEHICLE MAINTENANCE

In my maximum hustle days, I used to squeeze 7-10 signings per day into my schedule and drive 300 or 400 miles...daily, a few days per week. I had a 2005 Lincoln Town Car at the time (a gift from my fabulous grandmother), so it was like cruising around in a recliner. I loved it, and it made being on the road that long a very comfortable experience.

But driving that much takes its toll on *any* vehicle (Luckily Town Cars like to work!). The recommended oil change and service was every 3,000 miles, and there were months where I had to do that twice! Your vehicle is like your partner in this business. If any of your other tools break down, you can probably find a work around. If your car breaks down, you're out of business. While there are a few work arounds available, they are expensive and inconvenient. If your car breaks down, or is otherwise unavailable, consider: borrowing a car, renting from a company, or use Turo – like Airbnb, but for cars.

Get regular service on your vehicle and pay special attention to your tires. Take the time to build a relationship with a service facility you can count on when things go wrong.

I also highly recommend roadside assistance like AAA or AARP or others that may be include with your auto-insurance.

FUEL EFFICIENCY

Fuel efficiency is obviously important, especially when you're driving 300-400 miles a day. Keep in mind, not all of you will drive that much. I am a little on the crazy side when it comes to my business. I am big into the hustle and it's not for everyone.

As you can imagine, the Town Car didn't get the best mileage, but still not bad for an old boat. It got around 25 miles per gallon, and I still managed to thrive and enjoy the ride. With automobile technology today, it's easy to find vehicles that get 40-60 (or more) MPG.

If I could change one thing about when I got started, it would be to have a more fuel-efficient vehicle. But, the reality is, at the time, I had no options. I had no money, no credit, and no idea how big this would get. Start with what you've got.

CLEANLINESS

No need to get all OCD about this (unless you are already), but again, just remember that you are representing the closing agent and every professional involved in the transaction.

The inside of your car matters, too. There are some odd situations that pop up. You never know who may have to either sign in your car or see inside it when they hand you your phone, a pen, or something else you may have forgotten when you left.

Trust me, in this business, *lots* of bizarre, story-worthy, experiences pop up all the time.

EATING IN YOUR CAR

I am including a little section on eating because it *can* pertain to the cleanliness of your car. It can be a major challenge for mobile notaries and loan signing agents when we are on the road all day.

There are plenty of options for eating on the road. Fast food restaurants are everywhere, and an easy trap for us. They're cheap, fast and easy to eat. They also have obvious downsides, so please be careful on this.

Healthier options are springing up, like Mad Greens and Salad & Go. Substituting the typical sandwich or burrito for a healthy meal will serve you well.

Keep in mind that sitting in the car a lot is just as bad, or worse, than sitting at a desk all day. We have to stay active and eat consciously.

If our bodies fail, our mission fails.

MOBILE PRINTERS/SCANNERS FOR YOUR CAR

Believe it or not, they do make printers and scanners that are mobile, and with the right hook up, they can work in your car or trunk.

I tried this, once, and didn't really care for it. The main reason was, that the printer just never seemed to work right, especially for full loan document packages. It seemed to do okay for one-off documents, like one to five pages or so, but beyond that-very frustrating. In fact, I almost just chucked my mobile printer out on the side of the road on more than a few occasions.

Still, many people swear by these! When they work right, they might be super effective in helping you take advantage of more last-minute opportunities.

Same thing for the scanners. Some signing companies require fax/scan backs as soon as within two hours of the signing. Having a mobile scanner can help with that.

On the resources page, check out my interview with Notary Public Vernice King. She has a full office set-up in her truck. She shares the information you need to follow her example, if you choose to.

YOUR NOTARY BAG

If you're an office supply nerd, you're going to love this business. You can find all kinds of fun gadgets to make your business run more smoothly and efficiently. You'll have some items that are considered necessities, and then some that count as "luxuries." You get to decide which is which!

First, let's talk about the bag itself. Your notary bag is a briefcase, laptop bag, messenger bag, or some sort of satchel that you keep all your supplies in.

Ideally, this will be big enough to carry a few sets of loan document packages-legal size paper, too.

Having several interior and exterior pockets will help keep you organized. You may want a bag on wheels. A shoulder-strap may be okay with you.

There really is no right or wrong bag. Choose something that works for you and makes you proud. Clients will see your bag, so don't use a grimy bag with holes in it. This doesn't have to be a $200 bag, as you can find great satchels at the thrift stores, but you do want the bag to be clean.

My favorite bag, and I've been through a few, is the Kattee Crazy-horse leather briefcase 16" found on Amazon for around $130.

WHAT GOES IN THE BAG?

In addition to the supplies I mentioned before, there are a few things to consider having in every notary bag:

- File folders
- Spare jurats and Acknowledgments (State Specific)
- Stamp Ink Refills
- Hand Sanitizer
- More Pens
- Journal/Notebook
- Paperclips
- Jumbo Clips
- Daily Planner

AFTERWARD- PUTTING IT ALL TOGETHER

Having access to the information that can aid in our success is less of an issue than any other time in history. The answers, strategies, and advice to just about any question or situation exists on the device we touch an estimated 2,617 times per day.

We can read blog articles and books, attend seminars and workshops, hire consultants and coaches, take unlimited courses and collect various certificates. We are capable of learning just about anything. But if we do not implement that knowledge, we end up spinning our wheels-much like I was when I shared my story earlier.

Remember what GI Joe said, "Knowledge is *half* the battle." The other half is execution and implementation. The most effective way I have found to execute on my dreams and goals is habits and routines. Habits and routines are *everything*. They can also be difficult to put into place when you're self-employed or have tons of "distractions." In fact, if you're anything like me, there's even some resistance to having a routine in the first place. After all, isn't that what having freedom and flexibility is all about? So, we can sleep in when we want? Binge Netflix on a whim? Work in our pajamas?

As you tap into your vision, and your *why*, I think you'll discover that your real dreams and passions go deeper than that. Freedom and flexibility then becomes more than sloth and laziness. When you're really tapped into the impact you hope to make, and legacy you'd like to leave, you start to make different decisions. Just because you *can* binge Netflix all day, doesn't mean you do. You start to think and act like a champion-doing the things that champions do.

The irony is that those with the strict discipline and routines are the ones who enjoy the most freedom and flexibility.

FLEXIBLE SCHEDULE. UNLIMITED INCOME. LEGITIMATE BUSINESS.

How will the flexibility, limitless potential, and confidence-building legitimacy of your mobile notary and loan signing business serve you on the way to your dreams?

Being super clear about how this business "vehicle" will carry you to success will help keep you on track when the going gets tough. And, you can trust, it will get tough.

This book is your blueprint to get where you want to go. For you, you may have some different goals too. That's perfectly fine! Do what most people do not do and write down your big goal *and* the next 5 big steps that will get you there. Build this into the vision you have for your life and review it *daily*. This simple technique will differentiate you from 99% of your peers.

And, lucky for you, this book is laid out to give you your first five steps to get started as a mobile notary and loan signing agent:

- Step One: Become a Notary Public.
- Step Two: Get certified as a Loan Signing Agent.
- Step Three: Learn the Documents, Processes, and Etiquette.
- Step Four: Grow Yourself and Find Clients.
- Step Five: Manage Your Day to Day Business.

Think of each of these steps like buckets. These are the big steps that will "move the needle" on your dream of launching your business. Within each of those "buckets," there may be dozens of smaller steps to take to accomplish the big one. Again, this book demonstrated each of those steps in detail.

Now that you know what needs to be done, you have to make the time to do it. This is the difference in 1%'ers. Not only do they know what needs to be done, they schedule it into their day to make sure it does get done. No excuses.

Chances are, you have some distractions in your life right now. Maybe some other priorities, like kids, spouses, day jobs, sick parents, or any other number of things. The key is to carve out the time, anyway. Remember, you are not the only one with other "stuff." Many of the greatest people in history had "stuff," too, and they still made their dreams come true. Schedule this time for you. Might I recommend the morning?

Even if you are not yet a morning person, I recommend you implement a morning success routine that will advance you to your goals. That might mean waking up an hour earlier than usual, maybe even two hours early. Does that turn your stomach? If so, then I guarantee your dream isn't big enough then. Go back to it. Find a dream that, if it were to come true, you would practically jump out of bed every morning to make progress on it. That's how important this is! We aren't pitching a pipe dream here. You are being offered a vehicle that has the power to change everything for you.

If you work nights or something, adopt a success routine that works for you. Whatever time on the clock is your "morning," do it then.

When you plan your daily success routine, you'll want to balance it with the real practical, business action items, and the personal development components. This dream, or vision, you have for your life, will require you grow, or *become* the type of person that has, or does, those things.

The "becoming" part is often forgotten. It's what's happening while you're striving for more. It's hard to see along the way, but when you get there, wherever "there" may be, it will be obvious how you "became" who you needed to be in order to achieve the results you wanted.

GO AND GET IT

Don't let someone else's experience, or your history, define what is possible for you. This business, as a mobile notary and loan signing agent, can be the perfect tool for giving yourself the freedom to create the life you've always dreamed of. Own it, respect it, and commit to excellence. In a world that accepts, and even rewards, mediocrity, strive to deliver more than just ordinary results. Dare to be extraordinary.

If you're ready to take the leap, please join us in the Sign & Thrive Notary Training Course and Community. I am your Notary Coach and provide the complete system with *unlimited* mentor calls along your journey. Join us with a free 7-Day trial at www.notarycoach.com/course.

THE NOTARY IN THE ARENA

Adapted and Modified by Bill Soroka

"It is not the critic who counts; not the person who points out how the strong person stumbles, or where the doer of deeds could have done them better. The credit belongs to the person who is actually in the arena, whose face is marred by dust and sweat and blood and ink; who strives valiantly; who errs, who comes short again and again, because there is no effort without error and shortcoming; but who does actually strive to do the deeds; who knows great enthusiasms, the great devotions; who spends themselves in a worthy cause; who at the best knows in the end the triumph of high achievement, and who at the worst, if they fail, at they least fail while daring greatly, so that their place shall never be with those cold and timid souls who live in the gray twilight of existence, neither knowing the thrill of victory nor the agony of defeat."

—Theodore Roosevelt

APPENDIX: RESOURCES FOR MOBILE NOTARIES AND LOAN SIGNING AGENTS

- **Supportive Facebook Groups**
  - Safe Haven For Notaries
  - Notary Reviews: The Good, the Bad, and the Ugly
- **Associations**
  - National Notary Association
    - www.NationalNotary.org
  - American Society of Notaries
    - www.asnnotary.org
- **Conferences and Events**
  - National Notary Association Annual Conference
    - www.NationalNotary.org
  - Notary Symposium (California and expanding)
    - www.NotarySymposium.com
- **Training Courses & Coaching/Mentoring**
  - Sign & Thrive Notary Training Course and Community
  - Notary2Pro and Carol Ray
  - Laura Biewer at CoachMeLaura
  - National Notary Association

APPENDIX: THE SIDEHUSTLE LOUNGE- ADDITIONAL REVENUE STREAMS FOR NOTARIES

As a Notary Public, your options for adding on services, and even entire businesses, are wide open. There are some ancillary services, or niche markets, that go right along with being a notary. We will touch on these here. You can also get way outside the box on these, too.

I advocate for multiple streams if income, no matter what business you are in. This helps you accomplish your dreams faster, *and* it helps protect you against the downside risk in your business. For a mobile notary that focuses primarily on mortgage loan signings, the downside risk would be a slow down or halt in the housing industry. If loans dry up, your business dries up. By increasing your services and value, you can protect against this.

When you choose additional services or revenue streams to add to your notary business, be sure to choose something that is symbiotic and will work well with your day-to-day notary work. If you add services that draw too much energy away from your notary business, you may find this to be destructive to your overall plan.

Here are just a few ideas that your fellow notaries are using as a "side-hustle" to their notary business:

- Wedding Officiant
- Prepaid legal services Independent Representative
- Property Field Inspections
- Uber/Lyft Driver
- Legal Document Preparer
- Digital Fingerprint Service
- Process Server
- Apostille

GENERAL NOTARY WORK (GNW)

General Notary Work, or GNW, simply refers to just about everything else a notary does outside of the mortgage loan documents. This previously disregarded income stream can be a powerful addition to your overall business plan.

As I previously mentioned in Phase 1, each individual state, and even some counties, are responsible for the management of their notaries. In many cases, the Secretary of State, or the State's Legislature, is also responsible for setting their maximum fee a notary can charge for their services. In some states, this is as low as $1 per notary stamp, and in other states, it is as high as $20 per signature.

Across the United States, we are seeing a steady increase in these notary fees that finally make it very possible for a Notary Public to make a very comfortable, and sustainable, income by performing General Notary Work. In fact, when you effectively market yourself to niche markets as a notary, it is very possible to earn six-figures as a Notary Public *even* if you do not do mortgage loan signings.

THE RICHES ARE IN THE NICHES

Let's talk about those possible niches for a minute. There are thousands of different types of documents that the general public may need notarized, so we can't list all of them here. Still, each and every one of those documents is a potential niche you could target. If one person needs a certain document notarized, chances are, thousands more do, too. I'll list some of the most common documents below.

When it comes to general notary work, again, you will want to be very clear as to what your state allows and does not allow. In many states, a notary cannot provide the actual document that will be notarized. The customer, or signer, will need to have the document already in hand, whether from their own creation, or from an attorney that created it on their behalf. Additionally, some states do not even allow the notary to advise the signer as whether or not the notarization should be a "jurat" or an "acknowledgment." The notary can just offer an explanation of each, and the signer must make the choice. Many documents already have the necessary notary block information pre-printed on them, so you won't have to worry about it. But, in some cases, like when you are notarizing a handwritten letter, you may have to add the notary block.

COMMON GNW DOCUMENTS AND POSSIBLE NICHES

- Vehicle Title Transfers
- Power of Attorney
- Last Will & Testament
- Living Trusts
- Adoption Papers
- Divorce Papers
- Investment Roll Over Forms
- Medical Durable Power of Attorney
- Child Travel Documents

APPENDIX: MUST READ BOOK LIST

Whether you physically read these books or listen to them, won't matter. Listening counts!

If you're hustling this business the "right" way, you'll likely be spending a lot of time in the car. Optimize that time with audio books and you can earn the same education as a doctorate degree. This is your "Auto-University."

- *Professor Clossen's Notary Best Practices*
- *Notary Public Code of Ethics and Conduct*
- Your own state's notary handbook and/or state statutes
- *7-Levels of Communication* by Michael Maher
- *Superconnector* by Scott Gerber & Ryan Paugh
- *Miracle Morning* by Hal Elrod
- *Croissants Vs. Bagels* by Robbie Samuels
- *Lunching With Lions* by Katherine McGraw Patterson
- *LinkedIn For Personal Branding* by Sandra Long
- *The Motivation Manifesto* by Brendon Burchard
- *The Success Principles* by Jack Canfield
- *The Power of Now* by Eckhart Tolle
- *Six Months to Six Figures* by Peter Voogd

APPENDIX: REMOTE ONLINE NOTARIZATION

Remote Online Notarization, or RON, is approaching the tipping point in the U.S. More and more states have adopted legislation to legalize this all new "web cam" notarization, that removes the "physical presence" requirement.

Like any change, this new technology has sparked debate about whether or not this is a positive change. There is much conversation about fraud, jurisdiction, legality, and more. Still, the mortgage and title industry is embracing the wave-even leading the charge.

RON has been around, in one form or another, since 2012, and it is not likely to go away. I encourage all notaries to educate themselves on the legislation and processes surrounding RON in their state. Educating yourself doesn't mean you have to like it and use it. In fact, becoming a RON certified notary in your state isn't even a requirement. RON is just another level of service you'll be able to provide your customers…if you want to.

The key is to not tuck your head in the sand about RON. Learn as much as you can. Get dialed in. Make the best choice for you, your business, and your customers.

A great example of a Notary Public that immediately saw the opportunity RON has presented to the marketplace is Melissa Johnson Eldridge. I've asked her to contribute her story here so you can hear the perspective of someone else that realizes that this industry is *ripe* for innovation and initiative.

From Melissa Johnson Eldridge, M.S.

2017 my thoughts of a notary changed forever.

I used to think that notaries were always found at stores, banks, family friends, certain businesses, and courts. Now, you can find a Notary Public by mobile phone, and internet with an electronic and remote online/webcam session.

This is evolution! I became so fascinated! I started researching Notaries Public from Roman times, around 1693, up until today.

My mind vividly thought about the cave man evolution.

I was truly amazed and shocked it has taken so long for the notary industry to change. What's more is that even without significant change since the advent of the ballpoint pen, notaries have not only survived, but they've thrived.

Here we are in the 21st Century, in a time where we have converted home phones to cell phones, typewriters to laptops, gas powered vehicles to electric- and now traditional notary to electronic and remote online notary. WOW!

I thought, I want to embrace, experience, learn, teach, collaborate, and innovate. I want to be a part of this great evolution. I did my homework on RON. I became a customer for one leading company and because it was so new, I thought I would try working for one of the nation's leading companies and see exactly how this remote online notary work.

I had so many questions, and while there was little information out there for a consumer, or a notary, most of it left much to be desired. State statutes were vague, to say the least. It was challenging to find resources, information, education, and mentors on RON.

Being a full time teacher for 10 months of the year I thought summer would be perfect for me to get my notary business off the ground, and I wanted to start my business as an electronic notary with anticipation of July 1, 2018, being the day it would come into law in Texas.

Again, little did I know what it took to get an electronic/remote online notary business up and going. I had mixed emotions about it all, but after investing thousands of dollars, I just couldn't give up on it. A couple of months after joining the local Chamber of Commerce, attending networking events, and spending time on marketing, I received my first customer as an independent remote online notary.

I knew then this was more than just a quick I.D. verification and electronic signature gig. Remote online notarization is a customer service job. Customers had to be guided through the process of a Remote Online Notarization. This required patience, empathy, technical skills, and patience (did I say that already?). But it wasn't just the consumers that had questions and needed help.

The more I would advertise about RON, my fellow notaries would reach out for support. There was, and still is, very little specific training available for RON notaries. At first, I thought, *"Well, I'm still learning myself, literally from my own mistakes."*

Then one day a notary said to me, *"can you please take time out and teach me the basic concept of remote online notary?"* I thought again, I'm a teacher and a notary. Maybe this is something I can do. I felt her pain and passion and decided to offer her a one on one class.

This was the birth of my remote online notary training system. I have trained over 50 notaries within 6 months on basic concepts of remote online notary, and because it such a new wheel, I'm constantly learning and adding new concepts in each class.

Remote Online Notary is revolutionary and I'm still excited to be a part of it! Come grow with me as we grow into becoming the best Remote Online Notaries.

For more information on Electronic and RON training, please visit the resources page for this book.

CAN YOU HELP?

Emoji credit to Barbara Ray

Thank You For Reading My Book!

I really appreciate all of your feedback, and I love hearing what you have to say. I need your input to make the next version of this book and my future books better. Please leave me an honest review on Amazon letting me know what you thought of the book.

Also, as we commit to raising the bar in the industry, and encouraging in-depth and comprehensive training (no matter where you get it), I would appreciate anything you can do to share this book.
Thanks so much!

—Bill

ABOUT THE AUTHOR

Photo credit (and back cover image): Jennifer Denoia

Hi everyone! I am still a full-time mobile notary and loan signing agent based in Phoenix, Arizona. I love it here…usually. The summers are hot, and as a native to the state, I say every summer is going to be my last. Yet, here I am! I have my roots here, with friends and family. Plus, the winters are gorgeous and I can wear shorts and flip-flops year round. Hard to beat it! In addition to being a loan signing agent myself, I own a small signing company that facilitates signings in all 50 states. Plus, I own Notary Coach and have found a new passion in teaching and mentoring new notaries all over the country. I'll always be a serial entrepreneur, with multiple irons in the fire. This business allows me to do that with a certain focus because there is so much we can do under the "notary umbrella." That helps keep life fresh, interesting, and full of adventure. My favorite places to visit usually include water or mountains, and a perfect Friday night for me is a quiet one at home with a bottle of wine and a Golden Girls marathon.

Thanks for hanging out with me for a while!

Contact Me at <u>Orders@NotaryCoach.com</u>

Or

Book a FREE Mentor Call on my website <u>www.NotaryCoach.com</u>

Made in the USA
Columbia, SC
06 September 2020